To: Jerry and Di~
You are
Angels.

2 Do~

'21

All the Colors
of Green

*Finding nature's lessons
hidden in plain sight*

By Sharon Jordan Womick

Sharon Jordan Womick

PeaceLight
Press

ISBN: 978-0-9971661-6-3
Cover design by Amber Mabe
Book design by Chip Womick
www.peacelightpress.com
Printed in the United States of America

I dedicate this book to my husband, Chip,
who is the bravest man I know
and who stuck it out with me for 31 years
through times that would have sent many
(if not most) men running for the hills,
and without whom this volume
would have never come to be;
my daughters, Callista and Maia,
who have been two of my greatest teachers,
and without whom this volume would have never
come to be; my mom and dad, Marlene and Ken (RIP),
who taught me to be resourceful and creative and
think outside the box (mom); and to fall in love with
words and language and unspoken language and
things metaphysical (dad); without whom this volume
would have never come to be; and to all of my teachers
and all of their lessons — ALL of them — without
whom this volume would have never come to be.
And last but not least to the man and woman
who gave me passage into this physical realm.
Without them I would not be,
so it follows this volume would not be.

May we all be at peace
May we awaken to the nature of our own true lights
May we be healed
May we be a source of healing for All Beings.

Amen.

Sunday 15 August 2021

All the Colors of Green

CONTENTS

Preface

Behind all the colors of the leaves of green lie colors hidden, not yet seen.
When temperatures cool, and conditions are right, reds, oranges, yellows, a dazzling sight.

I was fascinated when I learned how autumn colors are hidden behind spring and summer greens and how it takes just the right conditions to allow the hidden colors to be seen.

When our daughters were young, I homeschooled them for several years. I slowed down, became more mindful, and joined them in the Kingdom of Childhood.

During those days, I started becoming aware of lessons (of sorts) all around us in nature, lessons that could be applied to other areas of life. I scribbled some of those ideas from nature on scraps of paper and stuffed them into an old briefcase. Nearly two decades later – when the girls had grown into amazing young women – I started writing newspaper columns based on the notes on those bits of paper.

They proved popular with readers. In 2017, my columns won first-place in the serious columns category in the annual contest sponsored by the N.C. Press Association. The following year the columns took second-place honors.

I stopped writing for a time, uninspired and unsure whether my musings were worth writing anyway. Then one day I came across a card a reader had mailed to me two years earlier. I had never read it. She had covered the card in stickers and had hand-crafted positive affirmation notes included with the card.

That reader inspired me to again see the good in the world and in my fellow man. I posted some of the columns that had appeared in print, along with some new material, in an online blog. Now, I am putting them in book form with the hope that others may also find meaning in the words I offer.

I am a mere mortal – flawed, and weird, and wonderful – just like everyone else. I spit. I burp. I fart. I cuss. I laugh. I cry. I am deeply spiritual, and every day attend the church that makes sense to me. I am merely the paintbrush (or the pen) in the hand of the creator, doing my part to bring things from the world of the unseen to the world of the seen.

With every word I write, I hope to move closer to living peacefully and lovingly on Planet Earth. I also hope that some who read my reflections on nature and life will awaken, as I did, to the true beauty in themselves and in the Kingdom of Childhood. If one person does, it will be worth it.

Sharon Jordan Womick
13 August 2021

There is an old Chinese story of a farmer
who had an old horse for tilling his fields.
One day the horse escaped into the hills.
The farmer's neighbors sympathized
with the old man over his bad luck.
He replied, "Bad luck? Good luck? Who knows?"
A week later, the horse returned
with a herd of wild horses from the hills.
This time the neighbors congratulated
the farmer on his good luck.
His reply: "Good luck? Bad luck? Who knows?"
Then, when the farmer's son
attempted to tame one of the wild horses,
he fell off and broke his leg.
Everyone thought this very bad luck.
Not the farmer, who said,
"Bad luck? Good luck? Who knows?"
Weeks later the army marched
into the village and conscripted
every able-bodied youth they found.
When they saw the farmer's son
with his broken leg, they let him off.
Was that good luck? Or bad luck?
Who knows?

We are created to be different.

Turn toward
the sun

I was greeted by one brilliant red rose when I pulled into my mother's driveway one late fall day.

Throughout summer her rose bushes had boasted blooms of palest pink, sultry purple, salmon tinged in magenta, and florescent red. The blooms faded in about a week, and the petals fell away.

A kaleidoscope of zinnias graced the side of my garden that year. I had scattered seeds of different varieties and let them come up as they would. They bloomed all summer, until frost. When I cut blooms for bouquets, they produced more.

Looking at that last rose of the season, I thought how odd it is that we are content with the different ways that flowers perform, but never seem to apply those principles to humans.

I believe all people at some time or other -- and some more than others – scurry around not feeling "good enough" or "worthy enough."

We think so-and-so's children are better

behaved, smarter, wittier. Someone at work always seems to do a better job or is more creative. Mrs. Smith can juggle full-time work and keep a "perfect" house. Mr. Jones is a more talented gardener.

We may become so caught up comparing ourselves to others we lose the ability to see how incredible we are as individuals.

What if we thought roses were performing poorly if they didn't bloom as long as zinnias – or that zinnias were lacking because their blooms were not as splendid as roses?

That seems ridiculous. Each type of flower is doing what it is supposed to do. We are content with that. Why is it so hard to realize people are being who they are supposed to be?

You might question this idea when it comes to people who drink excessively, or do drugs, or neglect their children, or ... the list of negative human behaviors is long. What about them?

They may be doing the best they can with what they have at that moment.

Sometimes flowers perform poorly because soil, fertilizer, water, and sun are important for healthy plants. Without the right amount of love, support, stability, and other "nutrients" the human organism needs, we too may perform poorly.

We don't give up on flowers. We try to provide the things they lack. Why do we so easily give up on other human beings and become so quick to judge?

Roses are not supposed to perform like zinnias and vice versa. Neither will perform well without the proper combination of things they need.

What if we thought of humanity as one big flower garden? Could we accept that some of us are, say, daisies, not roses, and not zinnias. Could we come to understand that not everyone gets planted in good soil, with the right amount of sunshine, water, and fertilizer?

Would that help us be more gentle with ourselves – and with others?

What if Mrs. Smith appears to juggle the world easily? Maybe she's a wild aster, capable of that. And maybe you're a peony, doing what peonies do.

It would be dull if all flowers looked alike. So it is with us. We are created to be different. And that's OK. But sometimes our expectations leave us dissatisfied because we do not bloom all summer like a zinnia or burst forth with magnificent, albeit brief, blooms like a rose.

I think of myself as a sunflower. I like to turn my face toward light. I am trying to accept that being the sunflower I am is good enough.

I try to remember that each of us has a unique path and to have more compassion and less scorn for those "planted" in poor soil, without enough light, water, or fertilizer. They have more obstacles. I think they may be braver than I am.

There may be those who are not content with being sunflowers. They may be trying hard to be roses. Or zinnias.

Perhaps if I stand here in the warmth of the sun, comfortable that I am at just the right spot – for me – they too may realize one day that being a sunflower is A-OK.

It was the effort that counted.

Teacher inspires 'Knobby Knees'

Phyllis Holland stood short in stature but tall in spunk and spirit. For more than 30 years, she taught in the Asheboro City Schools system, touching thousands of teenagers at South Asheboro Middle School (SAMS). She taught physical education and coached girls' basketball.

Holland died Feb. 10, 2015, but left behind a legacy of love, caring, kindness, and compassion. I was the recipient of her compassion in the early 1980s.

I was a gangly teenager, self-conscious about my long, skinny legs and huge feet. In elementary school, I had been called "Skinny Bones" and "Knobby Knees."

The first day of phys ed, Miss Holland covered expectations for the class. One rule: Everyone had to dress out in short, gray shorts and a drab gray T-shirt or be counted absent. My heart sank.

During my previous two years at SAMS, I was allowed to wear sweatpants that hid my "knobby knees." I tried to get another teacher but couldn't.

The first day, I did not dress out. I pretended to be sick and got a note from my dad. He wouldn't give me a note for the second session. I had told him I did not want to wear the gym shorts because they were too short. He said he did not think the shorts were the problem – and that my legs were fine. I sat out that class and took an absent.

Miss Holland asked me to stay after class. I explained my woes. She explained that I had to dress out. She assured me that if anyone made fun of me, they would get a demerit.

The next class, I dressed out. The last one out of the locker room, my face burned with embarrassment. I waited for the taunts. One boy in the class had picked on me in elementary school. He said nothing. No one did.

Later I learned that before I had come out, Miss Holland announced that if anyone made fun of anyone else, they would receive a demerit.

Soon I no longer dreaded dressing out. I still tripped over the basketball and didn't make the girls' team when I tried out. But Miss Holland asked me to be the manager. I got to travel with them and see my best friends, LuAnn Tatum and Amy Bell, wreak havoc on opposing teams. I felt like an athlete.

Though I still struck out most of the time in softball and sometimes tripped on the gym floor with nothing there, I actually looked forward to phys ed. Then it was spring and time for the annual phys ed "checkup."

My dread returned. I did fine on the sit-ups and running and (surprisingly) on the balancing tests. But the previous two years, I could not even get off the floor in the rope climb. I always got a zero on a scale of 1-10.

The fateful day came. I lingered in the dressing room thinking of just taking zeroes rather than humiliate myself again. But I decided that maybe this year I would manage to climb a little.

Sit-ups. 10. Running. 10. Balance. 10.

My turn on the rope came. My palms sweated. My hands and knees shook. I grabbed the rope, wrapped my legs around it and put my whole body into moving myself upward.

Nothing.

I redoubled my effort, wrapping my whole being around that rope, trying to will my body to move. Nothing.

I hung there for what seemed like forever, struggling, going nowhere. My face blazed red. I grunted and made a wildly uncoordinated attempt to "jump" my body up the rope. I heard snickers.

I let go and looked at the floor, waiting for my zero. The first thing Miss Holland did was give the boy behind me a demerit for laughing. It seemed like an eternity before she announced my grade.

10.

10?!!! I stared at her.

I got a 10, she explained, because she had never seen anyone put so much effort into trying to climb a rope. It was the effort that counted, she said, not the results.

People we meet who look worn, wrinkled, and gnarled might be the ones who have the most to offer.

The most ragged may be the best

As I sprayed and began scrubbing the once white plastic chair with more vigor, I thought to myself, "It still looks dirty." For a good five minutes I had been working on this chair that had started out mostly hazed with a green coating of the tiny plant life forms that had come to live on its surface during winter storage in a damp and shady spot. Now it was merely a dull gray. Scrub as I might, I could not get the gray to give way to the white that the chair had once been.

In my mind, if I could not get it back to white, it was not good enough.

There were 18 chairs to clean that day recently at my friend CL Hickerson's house. I offered to clean the chairs for the fire circle ceremony planned for later in the week. It was a crazy balmy near 80-degrees-day in February. A great day for playing in water. I even kicked off my shoes and socks, rolled up my sweatpants, and worked in a short-sleeve T-shirt, hanging my black sweat jacket on a fence to dance in the wind.

The wind gusted as the morning wore on and kept picking up in intensity, toppling over the lightweight chairs at times. The sky became more clouded. A cold front was approaching, and very nasty weather was forecast. I was working feverishly to get the chairs cleaned before the weather turned.

When I first looked at the rag-tag group of chairs I felt overwhelmed. Many had earth and leaves caked on them, and a layer of dirt sprayed up onto them through winter rains clouded their whiteness. Several had taken on the greenish cast, and most had dark stains in the seats where water had pooled.

I started with one. I just began work and decided not to look at all the others that eventually would need my attention. Just focus on one chair. I thought how I wished I could learn to use this approach more with all the things that seemed to call for my attention.

Focus on one thing and do it, rather than looking at the whole and becoming paralyzed and getting nothing accomplished. I made a mental note to try to remember that. Actually, that is how I am finally (after almost a year) sitting down and writing again.

I did not realize it at the time, but that was only one small lesson I would learn that day during three hours of spraying and scrubbing.

After about 10 minutes, I became frustrated with

my inability to scrub the gray off the chair.

"You need to get all these chairs clean," I thought to myself as I continued to labor. The chair simply would not give up its gray patina. Then, interrupting my thoughts of perfection, into my head flew a thought that made me break out in goosebumps.

"They cannot all be perfectly white. Some have more 'experiences' etched into their surface that, although on first inspection appear like dirt, are actually stains of many years and weathering many storms."

Huh? Was this about these chairs or about me and my own stains and scars I had been trying to reconcile? Suddenly I saw the chairs like humans.

They all had arrived shiny and white and over the years encountered various conditions that had altered their surfaces to varying shades from white to gray. The most stained and tattered had simply accumulated more "life experiences" than the others, adding to its chair "wisdom-ness."

I went on to another chair and then another. I sprayed each chair all over, top and bottom, and then began wiping the upper surfaces, the arms, the back, the legs and eventually the bottoms. Some came sparkling clean easily with one wipe down and a final spray. Some took a little extra wiping to get the surface dirt off, leaving slight stains here and there. And then there were the ones that took extra scrubbing and deep breathing and stepping back, rinsing, scrubbing again, stepping back, and realizing that the deeper stains and gray cast were good enough. They were clean. They simply bore the marks of their time serving those who visited fire circles over the years.

Finally, I got to the last three chairs and sighed. They were three of the most soiled – covered with greenish film from nearly top to bottom. Here at the end and quite tired, I had my three biggest challenges.

Aha. How often do we get to such a point in life and throw up our hands, feeling too worn out to do one more thing? I do often. Here was another lesson for me. Persevere, even when you feel the most ragged out. You may be close to a realization or a revelation, and if you stop you will never be gifted with its knowledge.

That was to be the case for me with the chairs.

I scrubbed and scrubbed. Finally two of them were clean, even though gray stains made them look dirty. But the last chair bugged me. It remained a deep gray and looked like it had not been cleaned at all.

I looked at the other chairs. Of the 17 cleaned chairs, several sparkled, brilliant white in the sunlight. Some had rose designs for their backs and even the creases in the designs had come clean. A few had some stains, but the original white showed through.

I resumed scrubbing the last chair but finally just

stopped. My rag was green and had holes worn in it. My hand felt numb, almost unable to grip the rag. I placed the chair with the others. It was a sorry sight.

Then I got all goosepimply again, and the following thoughts crossed across the window of my mind – yet more lessons from the chairs:

The work to bring each chair to its best possible state was complete. I had done what I could; it was time for me to rest.

When we are dealing with people, do we often exhaust ourselves trying to "fix" them to the point we think they should be?

We need to realize we have a part to play in their lives, but we can only do that part. We need to know when it is done and it is time for us to rest.

Some chairs almost exhausted my patience; some were easy. Isn't it so with people?

We are all teachers and students of one another. Many affect us. We affect many of them. Some have experienced a lot and may have a lot of "dirt and grime" caked on; for them to get back to a state of grace may take much work.

Some have not accumulated so much grime and clean up more easily. But they also lack the "experiences" that contribute to the richness of the stains and spots (and wrinkles and sags and scars) as the others.

But all can return to their state of grace with enough time and patience and encouragement.

We may be the water spray, or we may be the cleaning rag for another soul by a kind word or deed we offer. We may need to be the cleaning rag worn till it's full of holes. Others can be these things for us.

To return to our original shine, colored by the experiences of our lives is, for some, a rather easy and short matter. For others, it is trial by nearly getting our skins rubbed off.

It occurred to me that often the people we meet who look worn, wrinkled, gnarled, and otherwise not as well-kept by society's standards, might be the people who have the most to offer. They have experienced a lot in life to accumulate life's stains. Yet they are not the ones we are drawn to.

I was deeply pondering the ragged people idea when my friend CL, who had been working elsewhere in the gardens, walked up.

"Hey, CL. Which of these chairs would you choose to sit in looking at them as they stand here now?" I asked.

He paused, then pointed to one of the whitest chairs with a lovely rose design in its back. "That one."

Hah, my ragged people theory was right. People choose the shiniest chairs or people.

"Why?" I asked.

"Because I like the flowers on its back," he said.

"Not because it's the cleanest-looking chair?" I asked. He said he had not even noticed that it was one of the cleanest chairs.

"What about you?" he asked.

Without pause, I pointed at the last chair I had worked so hard on and which still looked dirty.

"I choose that one because it has experienced much," I told CL. "It may not look like much, but its shine, even through the gray haze, is greater than the others because truly it took so much more work for it to return to its 'state of grace.' Definitely that one."

CL smiled and stood quietly for a moment. "You know, most people, if they could choose, would never choose that chair."

And, I thought, what they would miss …

She handed me a butterfly, smiled, and walked into the store.

Betty LaGrange's unique ministry uplifts

"In the middle of difficulty, lies opportunity."
Albert Einstein

A woman has been spreading butterflies and paper angels, poems of inspiration, and other gifts of love around Asheboro for more than 10 years. One might think a person so inspired had enjoyed a life of ease and peace. But not so for Betty LaGrange, also known as "The Butterfly Lady."

LaGrange, who is 89, hails from rural New York state and grew up without electricity and running water. She married at 18 and had six children in 10 years.

Her oldest son had a rare bone disease as an infant. He was in the hospital for five weeks. When he was 6 months old, the doctors pronounced that he was the first person ever cured of the disease.

In 1958, this son was a gifted pianist at the age of 11. One winter's evening, he asked his mother to sit with him at the piano and play and sing

Christmas music. They sat for about an hour playing "Jingle Bells" and "Silent Night."

He died the next day after being hit by a car in a sledding accident.

"It leaves a hole in your heart," LaGrange said, "but with the Holy Spirit, he just rolls over and fills it up. I was always so glad I'd taken that time with him."

The night her son died LaGrange wrote a poem honoring him. Then she started a mission she continues to this day – writing poems for others who have lost children.

She and her husband, Sid, moved to North Carolina in 1996 to be closer to their children. LaGrange began crafting butterflies, an art she learned from a woman she met while camping. Her husband died in 2006, and LaGrange lived alone for three years before moving to Cross Road Retirement Community in Asheboro.

She makes the butterflies from old calendar page and says she's given out thousands. She also makes angels from coffee filters, origami birds, little gift boxes from scrap paper, and all sorts of creations using plastic mesh. She hands these out, too.

"Every once in a while, I give a butterfly out and the person says, "Oh, that's just what I needed today," LaGrange said.

Back in 2006, a butterfly was just what I needed. In 2006, I got my first "real" job since 1990 after staying at home and homeschooling our daughters. I had been out of the workforce for a long time, so when I was hired at an Asheboro store and had to punch a time clock, it was a bit of an adjustment.

I worked in the garden section. My main job was to keep the plants watered, no small feat in the heat of the summer. I had to drag a hose throughout the garden center and be careful to keep it out of the was of customers. It was exhausting.

One very hot day, one of my supervisors stopped to say he had received a complaint about wilting plants out front. Why had they not been watered? he asked. I explained I was working as hard as I could to get to everything. He told me to stop what I was doing and go out front and water. Then he told me my shorts were too short (for company policy) and walked away.

Tears concealed behind my sunglasses, I headed out front, lugging 200 feet of hose. At the garden center entrance, a woman stood watching me.

"God, not another customer with a stupid question to distract me from what I am doing," I thought.

She handed me a butterfly, smiled, and walked into the store. I was dumfounded. I looked at the folded paper creation with a magnet on the back and the words "God Loves You." I relaxed. I made it through the day, and my search for the butterfly lady began.

Finally, in February 2015, working on my first column, I learned who she was.

LaGrange had coffee and homemade banana bread when I met her to talk about her butterfly ministry. Her home was an oasis of peace. I left feeling that I had been in the presence of a real-life angel.

Toiling in the tulips:
Sometimes, just let go

My dad, Kenneth Wayne Jordan, died March 25, 2003. It was five days after his 69th birthday and just before the tulips bloomed. Tulips were his favorite flower.

When I was 16, he bought me a load of red dirt and I planted a bed of bulbs near the road at our house. I bought a collection from Michigan Bulb that had a lot of tulips. They bloomed faithfully for years.

The year he died I carved a circle out of the lawn in the front yard of my house in Ramseur and planted 25 tulips. By this time Cally! was 12 and also loved tulips. We added new tulips each fall from leftover bags we bought at a bargain after everyone else had planted theirs.

My favorite was one that was such a deep purple it looked like black velvet. We both were fond of a yellow streaked with red. Of course, there were the usual pinks and lavenders and the reds. I did not like any red flowers in my garden except for the red tulips and a red poppy that Mother Nature

25

planted in my front walk one season. After a few years, we enjoyed a kaleidoscope of color in the maybe 10-foot-diameter circle. We probably had 50-75 bulbs planted.

Over the years, fewer and fewer tulips bloomed. I dug up all the bulbs one year, amended the soil with leaves and compost, and replanted them. By this time Cally! had left for college. That next summer, even fewer tulips bloomed. I think there may have been 12-15. I asked around and learned that our resident squirrels – who I had seen in the bed – probably were dining on the tulip bulbs.

In 2012, I helped with a project at The Boys and Girls Club in Asheboro that was sponsored by Burt's Bees. We sculpted dirt (infused with wildflower seeds) into meatball-sized balls. They were called seed bombs. After they dried, you could throw them on hard ground and they would explode, scattering wildflower seeds in the area.

I "bombed" the tulip bed. That summer an array of wildflowers I did not know complemented the sunflowers I planted there for Chip every year.

I kept trying to rehabilitate the bed. To tame it. To make it grow the way I wanted it to grow. It proved to be a losing battle. Last fall, I pulled up the faux wrought fencing I had fashioned around the bed. It had come broken -- the plastic prongs that held it together were missing some pieces. I had gotten it real cheap. It was held together with electrician's tape.

The space was to be returned to yard in the spring, much to Maia's liking.

I pulled up the elephant garlic and transplanted it. A few tulips bloomed. I decided to just let them get mowed rather than move them. I did not have time to tend the space. Maia's boyfriend mowed our yard the first time this spring but did not mow the space.

Mother Nature took over. Rose campion of fuschia offset by silver foliage, 6-foot-tall mullein of velvety white leaves and the softest pink star-shaped flowers, fill the bed.

An unknown five-foot-tall plant with fluffy white, bloomed-out, dandelion-type flowers scatters its seeds in the softest breeze. Pokeweed growing berries for the birds stands un-hated.

The Artemisia Sweet Annie fills some of the empty spaces with the sweetest-smelling foliage waiting to be cut and fill summer rooms with a hypnotic fragrance. Stella d'Oro daylillies border one side, while glossy green soapwort fronts the bed.

There are more bees of all sorts in the bed Mother Nature created than there ever were when I toiled for hours trying to make the bed the way I wanted it. There is more color.

Recently, I stood transfixed by the wild beauty of this bed that has become itself. I realized that sometimes it is better to let things grow the way God and Mother Nature intended than to try to fashion them into what we want them to be.

"The Pedigree of Honey
Does not concern the Bee –
A Clover, any time, to him,
Is Aristocracy –"
Emily Dickinson
Version II
c. 1884

If I can be even half 'the man' you were, Dad,
my life will be well lived.

Lessons learned
from my dad

This Father's Day was the first that I have not cried looking at all the cards for fathers on display in department stores.
I didn't walk down those aisles. I didn't walk down those aisles because this was also the first Father's Day I did not buy a card for my dad since he died in 2003.There are 11 "unsent" Father's Days cards among my collection of cards. I like to send cards to people and write letters.

There is rarely a day that goes by that I do not refer to a little book that I gave my dad before his death and that my mom gave back to me after his death. He underlined portions on nearly every page. When unsure about a situation, I often consult the little book and read what dad underlined. Usually it gives me the guidance I need.

In honor and memory of my father, Kenneth Wayne Jordan, March 20, 1934-March 25, 2003, I would like to share with you the tribute I wrote to my dad three years ago:

I grew up in Asheboro and as a child loved tagging along with my dad whenever I could. I visited him at the hospital where he worked as a physical therapist. The department where he worked had shallow and deep steps, and I would hop up them on both feet, full of joy to get to see him.

On Saturday mornings, I would tag along on errands. I especially loved going to B.C. Moore department store downtown, where we would wander around looking at all the unusual and interesting items. In the summer, dad would let me go into Central Bakery barefoot because I liked how the cool floor felt on my hot feet. It was one of only a few businesses that was air-conditioned at the time.

During all this tagging along as a child, and later, when I was older and sitting with him on the screened porch at my parents' house – or after his heart attack, walking laps with him at Randolph Mall – he was always sharing this bit of wisdom or that – often in response to encounters on our journeys.

One bit of wisdom I try to remember is that all people are special.

"Always be kind to people," he told me. "Everyone has good in them if you listen deeply enough."

Years later he gave me a copy of a saying I still have on a wall. It says: "Small minds talk about people; average minds talk about events; great minds talk about ideas."

I would have to say the greatest piece of wisdom he gave me was a lesson on impermanence, although I am still working – nine years later – on grasping it.

My dad died of a sudden heart attack early in the morning, while sitting drinking his morning coffee and reading his meditation books.

A few weeks before he died, we were on the porch talking about death and the afterlife. He got up from the table, went inside, and came back with "A Manual for Living" by Epictetus, a book I gave him Christmas 2000.

He read to me: "Events happen as they do. People behave as they do. …Embrace what you actually get. When something happens, the only thing in your power is your attitude toward it; you can either accept it or resent it. …Therefore, even death is no big deal in and of itself. It is our notion of death, our idea that it is terrible, that terrifies us. …Don't dread death or pain; dread the fear of death or pain."

I know these lines precisely because my mom later gave me the book, and they were underlined.

When my oldest daughter, now 21, was nine, she was frustrated with me one day and told me, "You are the slowest to learn and hardest to teach mother I've ever had."

So I am.

It has taken me nine years to finally be able to make enough peace with death to talk about my father again. And, thinking about this, I remember another bit of wisdom he shared: "It does not matter how long it takes you to learn a thing, so long as you finally learn it."

If I can be even half "the man" you were, Dad – and still are – my life will be well lived.

You see, I am finally understanding something else you once told me: "Energy can neither be created nor destroyed, it only changes form. Just because the water evaporates, does not mean it's gone."

Smile may be what 'down on their luck' need

The man sat on the metal bench in the shade at the fountain at Bicentennial Park. He wore blue jeans and a T-shirt. His clothes were a little dirty, but it was close to noon, and I figured he was a laborer taking a break.

I sat on a bench across from him, enjoying the birds' songs and the slight breeze that made it tolerable in the shade that July day. Men and women on their lunch breaks in dress clothes passed by, going about their lunch-hour errands.

Our eyes met, and he smiled. I smiled back.

"It's a beautiful day," I said.

"It is a beautiful day," he replied. "A beautiful day to be alive."

We sat quietly for a few moments, and then he asked what brought me to town. I told him I had come to check on a booth I had in a local store and decided to walk around town while I was there.

He stood, walked over to my bench, sat down, and told me he lived downtown. He told me how he was an alcoholic and had lost his license, so

33

he rode a bike. How his daughter owned a local restaurant, and he had come to Asheboro so he could be closer to her. How he lived on the streets though because it was more peaceful than trying to live with other people. He smiled as he told me this story.

He did not appear to be drunk that day we sat and talked. I have not seen him since. I do not know if everything he told me was true, but I do believe the part about living on the streets was true.

I volunteered at Christians United Outreach Center (CUOC) for several months last year. I saw people lined up every day, waiting hours to get food. Everyone I dealt with was polite and appreciative. Several told me things they were doing to get back on their feet again.

I remember a couple of years ago, sitting around with a group of people talking about things going on in Asheboro. One of the members of the group started talking about how annoying it was when he walked downtown in the mornings and all the homeless people were lined up behind CUOC, which used to back up to Bicentennial Park. He went on to say that it ruined his nice walk to pass all those dirty people standing in the parking lot.

I was speechless. Those were people who needed help, for whatever reason. Substance abuse and mental illness are often contributing factors in people winding up needing assistance or living on the streets. Simply losing a job can land people on the streets.

When I see people who are "down on their luck," I do not see dirty people ruining my walk through Asheboro. I do not see people trying to take advantage of the system.

I see people who once had hopes and dreams and loves. I see people who are working so hard to just survive that they may not even know how to get help. I see people who have lost hope.

Sometimes, a smile, a kind word, or a short conversation for a person living alone is enough to bring that person back from the edge.

I talked to the man on the park bench for about 10 minutes. When I finally got up and said my "goodbyes," he told me he had thought he was going to have a rough day, but now he thought it was going to be a beautiful day. I hope he did have a beautiful day.

I know some of you are thinking, "Right, right, you talk to *those* people and you get scammed."

OK. There have been a couple of encounters over the past few years where I became aware that the person was trying to run some sort of scam. But those were a couple of encounters out of many.

As for me, I will still offer a smile, a kind word, maybe a conversation. And, if I have extra money, I have been known to buy a person a cup of coffee, too.

I do not know what tomorrow will bring.

Taking out
the large, gnarly demons

Early on the morning of Sept. 11, 2001, Chip wrote a poem for me. We were going through some difficult times. He wrote it before the horrible attack that occurred that day.

He wrote it two days before I was scheduled to go into a 28-day alcohol rehab program. I wish I could say that the 28-day program "cured" me of my alcohol problems. It didn't. Oh, it did for several years. Then I thought I had it all figured out. I could have a couple drinks now and then, and it would be OK.

It never was OK. I have the disease of alcoholism, and when I start to drink, I eventually drink more and more until it causes problems.

I wish I could say I only ever drank one more time after the 28-day program. I can't. I had to repeat the same pattern several times over. Each time the consequences of my drinking became greater.

On Jan. 26, 2014, I got a DWI. I thought that would never happen to me. It was a harrowing experience. It cost me a lot of money. I was embarrassed and humiliated. It hurt my family. It hurt my family just like all the other times I drank. I never meant to hurt anyone else.

I would start drinking thinking it would help me not feel so stressed. That it would help me deal with life more effectively. I always eventually wound up face down in the dirt. I would have to pick myself up, dust myself off, and face the destruction I had created. Often it took months – even years – to repair some of the damage. Some of the damage could not be repaired, and I have to live with that.

I read a quote once that said: "Maybe my sole purpose this lifetime is to serve as a warning to others."

That's kind of how I feel right now. I had another brief period of drinking this year. I thought it would help me cope with some very distressing life experiences. Luckily, I realized sooner than later that it was not helping, and I stopped drinking again. The distressing life experiences are still there to be lived with.

What I know for me is that if I do not drink, I have a fighting chance that large, gnarly demons will shrink to a size I can carry out with the trash.

Over the years I have read and re-read that poem that Chip wrote for me. A couple years ago Cally! hand-lettered the poem on a large poster board, and we had it framed. It hangs in our dining room

now. I read it several times each week.
It gives me hope.

Tomorrow Will Bring

I do not know what tomorrow will bring –
it is too bright to see beyond the horizon of today.
Yes, of course, I can see little snarly obstacles
waiting to trip me up
or weight me down with sheer numbers,
but these I am learning to step around
or to leap over.
When I do, they usually disappear.
And, yes, I see large gnarly demons
eager to eat me alive
or quash me where I stand, or as I run,
but these I am learning to look dead in the eye
and call by name.
They do not like it when I do this.
Then, they shrink to a size I can
carry out with the trash
or, at the very least, can bear
without breaking my back.
I also see the face of Spirit,
smiling,
always smiling,
on my brilliant horizon.
Her smile is warm and wide as daybreak
when I remember to count my blessings

and move forward,
sharing love.
Her smile is wistful and sad
when I am mired within myself
and walk in fear.
But Spirit smiles either way,
never relinquishing hope for me,
for she can see
the possibilities in my soul
even when I forget
they're there.

It's scary to jump.

Transfixed by the ant crawling 'round

The black ant crawled 'round and 'round the rim of the white enamel basin. First one way, then the other. In between, it would pause before switching directions again.

When I first noticed the ant crawling around the basin on our front porch, I figured it would soon climb down the side and be on its way. It would come to the edge of the lip on the basin like it was going to crawl under it and down the side but would stop and return to the safety of the top of the lip and go around again.

After several minutes I became intrigued, wondering how long the ant would continue to crawl around the edge, switch directions, and crawl the other way.

I finished my cup of coffee, certain that when I came back with a refill the ant would be gone. It was there but was still. It stayed still for several minutes. I wasn't sure if it had given up or if it was contemplating its next move – if ants do such things.

I got tired of sitting and watching the ant do nothing. I had things to do. Just as I was about to leave the porch, the ant starting crawling again. Around one way. About face. Back the other way.

Figuring this could go on all day, I was ready to leave again when the ant fell into the basin. I figured that was the end, that it would not be able to crawl out. But – surprise – it climbed one of the plastic bags in the basin and back onto the rim.

Maybe it was my imagination, but it seemed the ant moved a little faster around the rim now, coming out to the edge more often and appearing to look down.

Despite needing to get on with my day, I wanted to see what the ant would do. It seemed it wanted to get off the rim of that basin but didn't know how.

I told myself I would watch three more times around and then go. I remembered that a lot of the lessons I had learned in nature happened when I put the world on hold and just paid attention to what was going on around me.

I couldn't see any lesson in this ant crawling 'round and 'round the basin, but something made me wait. Even after three more times around. Even after so many more times around I quit counting. I sat there transfixed by the ant. The rest of the world fell away. I was in a sort of meditative state.

Just as I was feeling totally hypnotized watching this 'round and 'round, it happened.

42

The ant jumped!

It stopped in mid-stride, walked to the edge, and jumped. It did not look like a slip or fall. It truly appeared to jump. It landed safely on the ground and crawled away.

As I watched the ant crawl away, I thought about how many times we too get stuck crawling around the rim of a basin – stuck mentally or physically, going 'round and 'round, knowing some change is needed, but not knowing what to do.

It takes courage to leave the rim. It's scary to take a leap of faith. We might get hurt by the fall or get hurt by people who try to help by pushing us from the rim.

One thing is certain – if we refuse to leave the rim, if we just keep circling and circling, we will never know what other gifts we might have offered the world.

And we will never know if we flew or if we fell.

"Come to the edge," he said.
"We can't, we're afraid!" they responded.
"Come to the edge," he said.
"We can't, we will fall!" they responded.
"Come to the edge," he said.
And so they came.
And he pushed them.
And they flew.

– Christopher Logue

I was fortunate to stand there with my daughter in morning sunbeams, marveling at that spider web.

Maia and the orb weaver's web

One brilliantly sunny autumn morning Maia sat in the purple velvet chair by our bedroom window while I made the bed. We were chatting about this and that when suddenly she excitedly exclaimed, "Hey, mom! Come look at this!"

I hurried around to the window thinking it could be a rare bird that could fly away at any moment. There was no bird in the eucalyptus tree outside our window. Instead, there was an orb weaver's web that looked like it could measure nearly three feet across. Morning sunbeams glistened in kaleidoscopes on the silken strings. We sat mesmerized for several moments by its beauty.

"The spider is already gone," I commented, noting the hole in the middle of the web and no lovely, large, yellow-lined spider anywhere in sight. If the spider still resided in the web this was the time of day when she would be repairing the "holes" created by the previous night's catches.

We looked to see where her egg case might

be but couldn't see it anywhere on the web. I reminded Maia that often there were spider egg cases attached carefully just underneath the slight overhang where the shingles of our house met the brick foundation. We gazed at the web a little longer, and then we went about the day.

I didn't think of the web again until the next morning when I opened our curtains. I remembered the splendor of yesterday's web and eagerly anticipated seeing that beauty again. However, when I opened the curtains, there was only a single silken strand clinging between the house and the eucalyptus tree. I felt a pang of sadness for a moment before reminding myself that at least I had been able to see its beauty once.

Sometimes we miss things because we don't look at just the right time. We can get so caught up in our attachment to what we feel we must do to prove ourselves worthy human beings that we miss things right in front of us.

What if, on that morning, I had been in a rush because I had a to-do list a mile long and didn't know how I was ever going to get it all done? What if I had told Maia I would look in a minute, and she had taken it as lack of interest on my part and gone away, and I had forgotten to look?

I would have missed one of those increasingly rare opportunities to stand in wonder at nature with my daughter. Increasingly rare because she is no longer a child but a 17-year-old doing all the changing somebody that age does.

I was fortunate to stand there with my daughter in morning sunbeams – even if only for a few minutes – marveling at that spider web. I guess it's really cool she noticed it too – all the time we spent in nature when she was a child must have given her some connection to it although I sometimes wondered anymore with her life of computers and cell phones.

Here's the strange thing: Even though I experienced a beautiful moment with her, a happy time, I almost turned that happiness into a sadness when the web was gone the next day and I missed it. I wanted that happy feeling again. But I caught myself. I had once had the opportunity to experience the beauty we shared, and I needed to remember that, rather than longing for something I felt was lost to me.

Experiences, things, and events are fleeting.

They are here. They are gone. That is life.

I thought about that and how glad I was that I had taken the moment to spend there at the window with Maia. I held that good memory in my head while reminding myself that it was time for the spider and its web to be gone. It was a natural progression.

I also remembered a quote that one of Maia's friends once had on her social networking page. It said: "Don't let something that once made you happy now make you sad."

I smiled at the sun streaming through the window, opening my eyes to whatever new wonders I might see on this brand-new day and holding my happy memory in the forefront of my mind.

We get accustomed to things being a certain way.

Taking time to see the beauty in change

C hip and I have walked along a dirt road near our house for almost 20 years. Over the years, trees along the road have been lightly trimmed when a branch here or there hung too low. Town trucks and an occasional car were the only traffic the road got. It seemed to have become a forgotten road. It was more like a magical forest than a road.

Until a few weeks ago.

One morning the sound of chain saws and large trucks on the road made me walk out to see what was going on. I figured a tree had fallen, and the town was cleaning it up.

When I looked down the road, however, there were several trucks and people wielding chain saws. The people worked the rest of that day, with trucks going and coming, hauling off debris.

They were back the next day. And the next. They cut trees and vines and cleared undergrowth along half of the road to the bottom of a hill and then seemed to stop. Soon, however, they came

49

back and worked several weeks clearing the other half of the road.

Before the clearing began, when we entered the dirt road, it was like stepping into a canopied tunnel. In summer's heat, we looked forward to the noticeable drop in temperature when we walked up and down the shady road.

The first time we went out after the clearing, there was no noticeable change in temperature when we got to the road. The sun beamed down on the road. It did not feel like stepping into a forest wonderland.

I did not like it. I did not like it at all.

No trees overhung the road. Everything was cut back a good 10-15 feet from the road on either side. Large chunks of cement and other debris that had been used as filler along the sides of the road stood bare and ugly. It seemed the magic was gone.

When I voiced my dismay to Chip, he said he thought it looked nice. It was different, and knowing how very little I like change, he pointed out that with time I might be able to see the beauty in the new, cleaned-up look.

We walked several more times, and as we headed out, I dreaded seeing the butchered road. It still looked awful to me. I felt a sense of sadness for the loss of several trees I had admired over the years. A branch where a squirrel sat one season yelling at us when we went by was gone. I just could not see any beauty in it because I expected the old road – shady and secret and magical.

Finally, one day when we went out, I was caught off guard somehow. For the first time, I saw the road as it was. I wasn't expecting the old road. I was amazed at the transformation.

The road looked clean. All the falling-down trees on either side had been cleared, and strong, healthy trees swayed in the light breeze casting dancing shadows across the fallen leaves. At the bottom of the hill, two large trees stood almost like a gate. I had never noticed these trees before because of the tangle of overgrowth that had been in front of them.

When I stopped comparing the "old" road to the "new" road, I could see the beauty in the clearing that had been done. I imagined new wildflowers growing along the sides of the road in the spring now that sun shone on the road. Blackberries and honeysuckle would grow and eventually cover the pieces of cement.

How often do we do this in life? We get accustomed to things being a certain way and when they change, we cannot see the possibilities and beauty in the changes?

Chip was right. I did learn to see the beauty in the cleaned-up look. I just had to stop comparing the new road to the old road.

We will never know what we might be capable of if we don't begin.

Dare to begin: That's the hardest step

S ome weeks writing comes easily. Some weeks I sit in front of the computer for long periods of time rolling an idea around and around in my head with nothing coming together.

Like right now. I have been sitting here for close to an hour. I know what I want to write. It just isn't coming out of me right now.

What I have learned is that I must just start. And it's the "just starting" that is hard not only in writing but in other endeavors as well, as I was reminded over the weekend.

Sunday was a beautiful day, so Chip and I decided to go out and walk. We had not walked in nearly a month because of the weather. It seems it happens like that each winter.

It was hard getting started, and, once we got out there, it was like starting over again. The route seemed twice as long, and I felt creaky. My legs didn't seem to want to work. My hips and knees hurt as they usually do when we haven't walked in some time. It was hard. But we did it.

Every year it seems it takes longer and longer to achieve a level of fitness to where walking our nearly three-mile loop is invigorating rather than exhausting. Every year it takes less time to lose that level of fitness when we aren't walking.

As we walked, I saw daffodils already blooming. They had pushed up through cold winter ground to start afresh. Their yellow blooms swayed in the breeze. Do they bemoan the fact that they are having to start over year after year? No. They just do it. Aching hips and knees and all.

I saw some purple crocuses creating abstract designs in some grass. It was time to grow anew, so they just did it.

I wish I could be more like the flowers. I wish I could just start something easily when the time came to begin without thoughts that often hinder me – and sometimes even keep me from beginning. Thoughts like: "I want to write the best column ever. I want to jog again like I used to when I was younger. If I can't do these things, then it is not good enough."

Sometimes I try and try so hard to make things and do things so perfectly that I feel, over and over, as if I fail miserably.

It does not matter that I have put forth my best effort. It does not matter that I dared to begin.

The daffodils and crocuses do not think about things like how tall they will grow or how beautiful their blooms will be or any other concerns that might keep them from growing. What if they did and just decided not to grow one year because it was going to be too hard, or they might not be good enough?

That would be a weird spring.

What if we did not begin things because they might not be good enough? What if The Beatles or Dr. Seuss had not dared to begin?

Our world would be really different.

Maybe we won't write amazing songs or incredible books, but one thing is for sure. We will never know what we might be capable of if we don't begin.

Today I will stretch out these sore muscles and go out again to get some exercise. I may walk slowly, but I will be doing it. I will imagine the daffodils telling me things like "Hey! Way to bloom!" I find when I make things like a game, they are often easier to accomplish.

Who knows? I might even begin a couple other projects that I have been putting off because they seemed too large. All I have to do is get started.

Get started. That brings us back to the beginning of this column. All I had to do was begin and then ideas came together, and, in the end, I feel I have just written the very pep talk that I needed today.

I hope it inspires someone else to dare to start something they have been wanting to do.

Remember: The daffodils are rooting (no pun intended) for you.

When I can focus on what is, I handle things much better.

Worry won't help weather any storm

I awoke Monday morning expecting to see snow on the ground, just like many of you. When I looked out the window and saw absolutely nothing, I wasn't too surprised. Seems the weather people didn't quite get it right.

Schools were canceled, and the roads were salted – just in case. Everywhere you went people were talking about the weather and speculating what might happen and whether they would be able to get to work. The weather forecasts kept changing the lines of where different types of precipitation might fall. Nothing was certain except that there was a whole lot of worrying going on.

Over the weekend people had stocked up on the essentials – milk, bread, and eggs. I joked with a cashier at the local grocery store about how it seemed people planned to live on French toast during a storm.

I was buying a gallon of milk. It had nothing to do with the forecast. I was just out of milk.

Looking back over the years, there have been

times we did prepare for impending storms. We would stock up on groceries, fill our kerosene containers, make sure we had fuel for our Coleman stove and that our flashlights worked.

Preparing was productive.

The worrying I did was not.

Sometimes I would worry and fret for days about what might happen: What if we can't get out for days? What if our power goes out? Do we have enough kerosene to stay warm? Will all our food spoil?

The worry train of thought would go on and on.

Then we would get just a little snow or none at all. All the worrying about what might happen had been needless and in vain.

How often do we do this in our daily lives? We worry about this and that, what might happen, what could happen? Does it help us weather the storms of our lives when they do come – if they do come?

I have found that worry does not help me at all. It can be paralyzing.

Back in 2000, I prepared for Y2K. Yep, I got us ready for the possibility of the end of it all. I nearly drove my family crazy with my worry about what we would do if it all ended right there when the clock struck midnight on Dec. 31, 1999.

Nothing happened.

Everything went on just as it had been going on. But guess what? When the big winter storm of

2000 hit a couple weeks later – dumping nearly two feet of snow on us -- we were ready.

If you remember, the meteorologists totally missed that one. Many people did not have time to prepare. Many people had no time to worry. We survived anyway.

Many times I worry about storms that never come. When I get blindsided by an unexpected storm, I have no time to worry. Really, if you think about it, worry doesn't help anything at all. When I worry about a storm that never comes, I miss part of my life all caught up in worry.

None of us, not one, knows when or where the next storm will blow into our lives. When I can just focus on what is, and deal with that, and then move on to the next thing when it happens, I handle things much better.

When I do get all bound up in knots worrying about something, I think of a little saying I saw somewhere that helps me get things back in perspective: "Worry is interest paid in advance on a debt you may never owe."

Enjoy the little things; they are big things

The tiny flowers start appearing in the grass this time of year. Flowers most of us would call weeds. Flowers many of us would not even see.

I would not see these tiny flowers either except that many years ago two little girls brought them in by the handfuls. Now each spring I see faint white and purple in the grass, and I smile.

A collection of small glass bottles of cobalt, light blue and clear – bottles that once held medicines and colognes -- still line the kitchen window. They still serve as vases for the tiny flowers I still bring in each early spring.

We called it our kitchen window garden. An occasional dandelion would brighten the window garden. We always thrilled watching as the yellow flower would transform into its puffy white seed head right there in the bottle of water. Sometimes we would take the dandelions outside and blow their seeds all over the lawn to grow new flowers the next year.

61

I have a little wooden box I bought at a flea market that sits on my bedside table. On the top it says: "Enjoy the little things in life, for one day you will realize they were the big things."

Little wildflowers brought in by little hands was a little thing I did cherish. I still do cherish. I am glad I did not just lay the little flowers the girls had gathered aside to wilt and to go out with the compost. I am glad that I was aware that something quite amazing was happening. That this little thing really was a big thing.

The tricky thing about the little things is that sometimes, when they are happening, they do not seem like anything special. No awards or ribbons or trophies are being given.

If we are not careful, we miss them altogether. Sometimes life's distractions keep us from being present in the moment and really paying attention to what is going on around us. We miss little wildflowers in the grass.

When I saw the little flowers in the yard this week, I started thinking about the kitchen window garden and then about other little things that truly were (and are) the big things.

These are a few of the little things that have been some of the truly big things in my life:

It is a warm summer afternoon, and a small plane is flying overhead as I run barefoot through the backyard to help my mom take laundry off the line. I loved helping her gather the fresh-smelling clothes that would fill the bedroom where we folded them with their outdoorsy smell.

Even now when I hear a small plane flying overhead I get the happy feeling I used to get helping mom get the laundry in off the clothesline.

Years later, warm summer days could find me and the girls walking through the woods to the river. We often waded out to a small island where there was a rock shaped like a couch.

We would sit on the couch rock for long periods of time with the sun warming us, just watching and listening to the river.

There was the time we bought a butterfly kit and watched as the five caterpillars morphed into five chrysalises and then eventually emerged as five painted lady butterflies. We released them on our yellow butterfly bush. Today when I see painted lady butterflies around the yard, I imagine they are descendants of the five we released.

Then there were the elephants and unicorns, dogs and cats that we would watch romp across the sky when we lay sprawled on the lawn watching clouds float by.

I remember gathering each evening as Chip read the Harry Potter books aloud. I think about gathering with family around tables sharing wonderful meals. I look forward to hot cups of tea on the front porch with Chip in the afternoon.

Now that I have started thinking about it, there are so very many little things that have brought joy to my days over the years.

And yes, I do believe the little things really are the big things.

Have faith; acts of kindness deliver in time

Several months ago, I arrived home one very cold night to find a cat meowing under one of the cars in our driveway. The cat came out when I called and let me pet it. I brought it up on the front porch to eat. The next day it was gone.

Over the next few weeks, the long-haired calico would visit the food dish on the front porch every now and then. We figured she was a female, since almost all calicos are female.

We also figured she belonged to someone because she was very sweet and loving.

As the weeks rolled by, and she began frequenting the food bowl more often, I started wondering if she could be a stray. I asked neighbors on the street if she belonged to them, but no one claimed her.

Eventually "Calico" would be on the front porch in the morning, sitting on one of the chairs waiting for breakfast. She would leave during the day and often be back at night.

Maia made a basket for her during one

particularly cold period, and later I put a cushion on the table on the front porch. She started sleeping in the basket, and some days would sit on the cushion sunning.

Her fur got longer and thicker, and she began putting on weight. We thought she was just putting on a winter coat and getting enough food to eat. One day I picked her up and realized her belly was really large.

She was pregnant. Really pregnant by the feel of it. It was mid-February. What would happen to kittens born in the dead of winter?

Chip and Maia and I discussed the situation and decided we should provide some sort of shelter where she could have her kittens. I got a large box from the grocery store and with some modifications fashioned a cat box lined with quilt batting and towels.

She would not go into it. I tried putting her in it. She would run out. She would sit on the cushion right in front of it, but that was it. For about two weeks, she ignored the box.

I felt like making the cat box had been wasted effort. I almost decided to remove it.

A little more than a week ago, I went onto the front porch one morning to put out cat food and have my cup of coffee. There was no sign of Calico, which was odd because at this point she was on the porch every morning. I figured she had gone off somewhere to have her kittens.

I had not been sitting there long when I heard the faintest mewing sound. At first, I thought it was a bird. Then I realized it sounded like a kitten.

Sure enough. When I looked into the box, there was Calico and five little kittens. Building the cat box had not been wasted effort after all.

I built the box because it was the one thing I could do to try to make life easier for Calico. I had no control over whether she would use it or not.

I think sometimes when we offer a helping hand or kindness to the people or creatures we meet, it may seem like it makes no difference.

We build a box, and it's ignored. We build it anyway because we want to help. Then we have to be patient. We want the cat to go right in. She doesn't. We have to have faith and wait, knowing that we have done what we can. Whether the cat uses the box or not, we did what we could to help.

We put forth the effort and try not to be attached to the results.

Now that Calico has pretty much taken up residence here, I know the next thing I will do to make life easier for her in the future. I will get her spayed, once the kittens are weaned, and we find homes for them.

For now, we are enjoying peeking in the box and watching as the kittens grow. And I am glad I did not remove the box when I did not get the immediate response I expected.

Face challenges:
'It's a piece of pie'

He said, "It's a piece of pie."
I thought about my attempts to quit smoking. I wasn't feeling at all like it was "a piece of pie." I was feeling like I stood at the base of a huge mountain, one I had tried to climb before and had fallen off over and over.

I felt paralyzed.

I had tried to quit smoking so many times and in so many ways that I felt I had exhausted all possibilities. I felt like a failure.

I knew this mindset was counterproductive. I knew thinking how hard something was going to be only made it harder. I had proven that to myself just last week.

For several weeks, I have been playing online games that challenge the brain. Some of the games are really difficult for me. I started playing only the games that were easy. When I did play one of the more difficult games, I would go into it dreading how hard it was going to be.

I did not perform well.

One night last week, I sat down on the couch to play the games. The television was on, so I was slightly distracted. I wasn't thinking too hard about the games I was playing and scored out the top on the easy games.

I decided to try some harder games, not really thinking about them or how hard they usually were. I made my highest scores on those, too.

I was surprised. It was as if something in me had been freed when I relaxed and played rather than being stressed about how hard it was going to be.

I stopped thinking about how I had performed in the past and just played. Some of the harder games actually became quite enjoyable.

This got me to thinking about games and lessons we have in life.

How often do we avoid the ones that are difficult or challenging? We get it in our heads that this game or that lesson is too hard, so we shy away from it.

Maybe we have tried a game and done poorly. We begin to think we will never perform well or understand the lesson. We avoid the very things that may help us grow and improve the most.

Sometimes we need someone to help us understand lessons we are trying to learn or to accomplish what we are trying to do. Someone who helps us take those first tentative steps up the mountain until we have the confidence to continue on our own.

I had a hard time with math in high school. Math totally stressed me out, so I had to seek help. My math teacher and my dad worked extra with me to help me understand the concepts.

Life lessons are not always so simple as learning math. We may have to learn to live with a serious illness or the serious illness of a family member. Maybe we have a loved one with a mental illness or substance abuse problems. We may struggle with trying to lose weight or quitting smoking. The list goes on.

These are the things that challenge us and that can paralyze us.

These are our difficult games.

The tough lessons.

I want to quit smoking. I may feel I have failed, but I haven't, because I have not given up. It is time I seek help from someone who helped me quit before and who can help me up that mountain.

When I played the online games and aced an easy game, it was no big deal, but when I did well on a harder game, I felt a sense of accomplishment and new confidence in my abilities.

So it is when we embrace life's challenges.

I cannot even imagine what it is going to feel like when I can say I am 30 days smoke-free. Or six months. Or one year. But I cannot wait.

It's going to be a "piece of pie."

Putting pieces back together is what counts

The woman said, "Sometimes the pieces don't go back together the way they were before."
There she stood, poised and smiling. I never would have thought that at one time the pieces of her life had lay about her, broken.

She was raped in college and spent years trying to go on with her life before she realized her life had been changed forever. She got involved in advocacy work and slowly began to heal. She reassembled the pieces of her life into something different, more beautiful, and stronger than before.

I was cleaning in the kitchen and ran across a mosaic trivet one of the girls made years ago. I had never really thought much about the trivet, but, as I cleaned it, I noticed how its beautiful pattern had been created from odd bits of tile.

All nine of the pieces had at some time been part of other things. Odd shapes in blues and burgundy and brown. They had been assembled into an attractive piece of art with cement and a little creativity – broken pieces coming together to make something new.

This made me think of a song from back in the '90s. Part of the lyrics were, "I may crack, but I'll never shatter." But sometimes we crack. Sometimes we shatter. The pieces of our lives lay scattered at our feet, and we feel as if everything we once believed to be true has been destroyed.

Maybe it's the end of a relationship, a terminal illness or the death of a loved one, drug or alcohol addiction, mental illness, or being the victim of sexual assault or other acts of violence.

These things rock our worlds. They leave us standing looking at a world we once thought we knew, and it no longer looks familiar.

I believe that these times that try our souls are not meant to destroy us. It may feel like we have been destroyed, but really it is an opportunity to rebuild ourselves into something new.

It may feel scary, but it can be done.

We may stand frozen for periods of time, looking at the broken pieces and wondering how we are ever going to make sense of any of it again. Wondering if the pieces will ever come back together. Wondering how we will go on.

We start by picking up those pieces and working with them. We need to be patient and have faith that it can be done. We need to find the right glues and cements. We may need to enlist the help of others.

Many years ago, we came home to find our Christmas tree lying on the floor. It may have been that the weight of the ornaments placed mostly on one side of the tree had toppled it, or it may have been that one of our cats climbing in its branches brought it down.

When we lifted it, several glass ornaments lay in pieces. One was a handmade glass ornament with an angel painted inside. It had broken into many pieces. I thought it was lost, along with several plain glass ornaments that had shattered.

As I started picking up the broken glass, Cally!, who was seven or eight, said to let her have the broken pieces of the angel ornament. She said she could glue it back together.

I doubted it could be fixed but got her some glue and let her gather the pieces.

Several hours later she walked into the kitchen holding the ornament. It looked like nothing had ever happened to it unless you looked really closely – then you could see tiny cracks.

Maybe the shattered or jumbled pieces of lives in disarray will go back together with just a few cracks that add character, or maybe they will come together as something entirely new, like a beautiful piece of mosaic art.

But, if we believe they can, and we do the work, they will come back together.

We still hang that ornament on our tree every year. We hardly ever notice its cracks anymore.

Sometimes cleaning out gives us breathing space

It was all I could do not to get out of the car and go pick up the large stuffed bear that lay in the area outside the building where people dump discarded items at the county landfill.

It wasn't my bear. It had fallen off someone else's vehicle as they backed into the building to unload items they no longer wanted. They unloaded their stuff and drove away, leaving the bear lying there.

Someone had once loved that bear.

It was a great bear.

When my mom saw the bear fall off the vehicle, she immediately told me I could not go get the bear. She knows me well. Over the years I have dragged home all sorts of other people's discards thinking I would one day put them to some useful purpose. The attic is full.

We had brought a load of stuff to the landfill that I had piled in our side yard. After we unloaded the items -- some I would have taken back home had it not been for mom -- our car wouldn't start.

77

It wouldn't start even after we tried to jump it with the help of a nice man who had been unloading beside us. He helped us roll it out of the bay and across the lot, where we waited for nearly two hours for AAA. We got to watch as an almost continuous line of vehicles came to get rid of an unbelievable number of unwanted items.

As I watched load after load of items being dumped at the landfill, I realized how much stuff people accumulate and eventually have to throw away. I realized how very hard it was for me to throw things away.

I attach memories to things. It is as if when the thing is gone the memory will be gone too.

I kept looking back into the building where we had dumped our stuff, thinking about going back in there and pulling a couple of things out. I watched as the two white plastic chairs we had dumped got scraped into a huge pile of junk.

They were broken beyond repair, but a part of me wanted them back. They reminded me of long summer days sitting in the yard and summer parties. The broken-down bicycle reminded me of teaching the girls to ride a bike.

The cars and trucks pulling in drove around the bear until finally the man working in the building drove out on his piece of machinery, scooped it up, took it into the building, and dumped it on the pile of discarded items.

I kept thinking of something mom always told

me during spring cleaning when I was growing up: "You have to get rid of the old to make room for the new to enter."

Finally a man from AAA came and jumped our battery, and we drove away leaving chairs, bike, bear, and other items behind. I felt sad, as if I were leaving part of me in that rubbish pile.

But I felt better when we got back to the house and pulled into the driveway and looked out over a side yard no longer piled with broken-down items. I could breathe easier.

And I still had memories of the good times some of those items had held for me.

I realized that sometimes getting rid of the old does not mean something new has to come in and take its place. Sometimes clearing out just gives us breathing space. It gives us space to enjoy the items we still have that serve a useful purpose.

I have saved all manner of materials, from furniture to odd bits of this and that. I have done this because I believed that, one day, they might be used for something. In the meantime, stuff piles up until – when the time comes that something is needed – I can't find the item I know I have somewhere.

I think it is time to do some more discarding.

It may feel scary, but I like having more breathing space – and being able to find things when I need them.

*We try to teach them what they need to know,
and then we have to let them go.*

Mama cat (and parents) do their best to teach

This will probably be the last column I write about our kittens. It will be the last one because our kittens are about ready to go out into the world. It's going to seem lonely on the front porch once they are gone.

It has been quite a journey this past six weeks watching them grow from little furballs oblivious to the world outside their box into rambunctious little cats playing all over the porch and spilling into the front flower bed.

The stray mama cat who chose our porch to have her kittens is weaning them. She gets up on a chair or other high place as much as she can to keep a watchful eye without being nursed.

It's been like having a new baby in the house. We have watched and laughed as they scamper around bowling each other over and as they sidestep each other with little arched backs. They have been photographed and videotaped a lot. We have done the best we could to protect them.

We put cardboard all around the side of the

porch we blocked off to keep them from venturing into possibly dangerous territory.

One night we came home, and two kittens were missing. We found them off the porch, huddled against the house with mama cat, who apparently had carried them off.

We put them back on the porch, and luckily mama let them stay. It rained later that night and the place where they had been flooded. Mama cat had some good reason for moving her kittens, even though it was not the best choice at the time.

In our lifetimes, we, too, make choices for our children that we think will be the best for them, only later to realize that maybe they weren't the best choices after all. Despite our best efforts we make mistakes.

After a while, the kittens began escaping on their own. We kept putting them back into the blocked-off area and adding rocks and boards to try to keep them in. Eventually we just had to open the area, and let them have free reign of the porch.

Sometimes we try so hard to protect our offspring that we forget to trust in the divine unfolding of life. We forget that things happen exactly as they should and when they should, even if we do not understand at the moment.

When we started putting out wet cat food for the kittens to start eating, we also put out a litter box. I watched as mama cat showed the kittens how to eat the food then got in the box and showed the kittens how to use it.

I am not sure she had ever used a litter box before, but she figured out what it was for and taught her kittens.

Sometimes we teach our children things that we never learned because we want them to have the skills that we never had but that will help them when they go out into the world.

Mama cat has brought a bird and a chameleon to her litter and tried to show them how to hunt. I am not sure they understood the lesson, but mama cat tried.

We do that with our children. We try to teach them what they need to know to be safe in the world. Then we have to let them go.

Five little kittens frolic in the flower bed. I will do my best to find them good homes where they will be spayed or neutered, so they do not wind up a stray on someone's front porch. I will get mama cat spayed.

I will do my best and then trust that everything will work out OK in the end.

Your gift
can change the world

Our daughter Maia worked at Just Save in
Ramseur for four years. She met many
people she would often see out at various
places. They would always smile and speak to
her, and she would talk to them, offering them her
smile that can brighten a room.

She would occasionally come home and mention
difficult customers, but there would always be
someone that day who had done something
to offset whatever unpleasantness she had
encountered.

There was the man who would come in early
and buy a newspaper on the way in and leave it
with her to look at until he checked out. The man
who would buy multiple packs of gum and open
a pack and leave some for the cashiers when he
checked out. There were customers who gave her
a piece of fruit when they checked out.

Each of these acts positively affected her day,
even if the people did not realize the impact of
their acts of kindness. They made her feel happier,

and she shared that happiness with the other people she encountered.

When Maia turned in her notice, customers heard she was leaving and said they would miss her. All those years she had been sharing kindness with them through her kind words and smile.

A few days before her last day, a man who she had gotten to know told her how sad he would be to see her go. He told her she had shown him kindnesses that he had never expected.

One day when she was on the way home, she had seen him walking along with his groceries. She stopped and offered him a ride. She gave him a ride on a few occasions. It was just a little more than a mile but carrying bags of groceries makes that distance seem much longer.

He wanted to give her a card, but told her he didn't have the money to buy a card. She told him to just make her a card.

On her last day at the store, he came in and handed her a handmade card. He had fashioned an envelope using two pieces of notebook paper taped together and had drawn designs on it.

The card inside was a sheet of notebook paper on which he had written:

Maia,
Just when I thought my heart had too much scar tissue to feel ... you leave.
Recall the end of 'The Wizard of Oz.' I know how the

tin man feels.

Sometimes a heart has to break to remind you that you still have one.

I'm proud of you, Sugar. Spread your wings and soar, sweetheart – our country needs a new eagle.

Stay sweet,

_____

When Maia came home that day she was very touched by the card. When she read it to me, tears welled up in my eyes. I was so proud of her for being the kind person that she is. I was touched by how she had impacted the life of this man.

The man thought he had to have a store-bought card, but what he created far surpassed anything that could have been bought.

Sometimes I think we hold back offering kindnesses to others because we do not realize that what we have to offer is "good enough." We might think we need to offer something grander or fancier than what we can offer.

This makes me think of a song called "The Gift."

In the song an orphan, Maria, does not think she has anything to offer at the Christmas Eve gift-giving service for the baby Jesus. All she has is bird with a broken wing that she rescued. She waits until everyone is gone before she takes her bird in its small cage. She does not think it is as good as the diamonds and perfumes others have brought.

After she places the bird with the gifts, she opens the cage. The bird flies from the cage and begins singing a beautiful melody – the very first nightingale's song.

A smile, a kind word, a bird's song can change the world. But not if they are not offered to the world.

Cut knees not meant to stop us from running

I sat mesmerized as one of the most beautiful renditions of the song "Taps" I have ever heard filled the church. The father of a dear friend had died. This was his celebration of life ceremony. He had embraced life and offered his gifts freely to the world.

Dick Peterson had undoubtedly encountered sadness and sorrow in his lifetime, but he continued to offer his special gifts to the world in 4-H and many other community events.

He celebrated life.

Listening to "Taps" took me back to summer camp in the North Carolina mountains. Each evening we would climb up the mountain to the top where we sat on benches overlooking the valley. We would have a service giving thanks for the day we had enjoyed. At the end, "Taps" was played to say goodbye to the day ending.

One evening I took off running down the mountain and fell. I cut my knee badly on a rock. I never again ran that freely down the mountain.

But I still climbed it and came down each evening.

As we pass through life, things like cut knees happen that can stop us from running down hills anymore. A bruised elbow here, a sprained wrist there, and soon we can start feeling battered, rather than inspired, by life.

We may start feeling like we are just surviving. We forget to look at the stars in the night sky or no longer take our shoes off to feel the cool grass and earth beneath our feet.

When the girls were born, I made posters welcoming them to Earth, based on a poster I had seen in a catalog by an artist named SARK.

The posters read:

Welcome to You! Who came through the door of the soul. You are a radiant dreamer … Bless this child with: true love, angels, rainbows, surprises, amazing faith, pure laughter … You're so beautiful, and everybody loves you! You are deeply wanted. We're so glad you're here! Bless you. How do you like Earth?

What if we could each carry this blessing with us through life? If we could remember that both happiness and sorrow will visit, and it's all a natural part of this thing we call life. If we could remember that we are all wondrous creations.

We all will have our versions of cut knees, of losses, and of sadness in this lifetime.

We all will have joyful times – falling in love,

the birth of a baby, seeing rainbows, the return of spring each year.

Cut knees are not meant to stop us from doing the things we came here to do. They might slow us down, make us a bit more cautious. But we still need to climb up and go down mountains. We still need to offer what we can to the world.

We are each unique and unrepeatable. There never has been, nor will there ever be, anyone else just like any of us. No one else can offer exactly what each of us can to the world.

This reminds me of a story I read once. It said that if the Universe were as big as the ocean, and if there was a single wooden ring floating on the surface of that ocean and a single turtle swimming around, the chance of getting a human birth would be the same as the turtle surfacing with its head in the wooden ring.

During Dick Peterson's service, one of the pastors told the congregation that this life is not meant to be a proving ground; that it is an opportunity to have a joyful response to the privilege of living our lives.

Our unique and unrepeatable lives.

As Dick Peterson did.

Amen.

Change your view: See beauty in unexpected places

I have never been a fan of fake flowers. Plastic and silk flowers have always seemed pointless to me. They lack the energy of living plants. They do nothing and need no care.

During the flowerless winter months, I always miss the flowers of summer and at some point wish for just one flower to brighten a gray, rainy winter day. This past winter my wish came true because my opinion of fake flowers changed.

I was driving in Asheboro one drizzly day and feeling particularly bleak. It was cold, and it seemed everything had taken on the gray cast of the day. As I drove down a street I rarely travel, I passed an apartment building where flowers of all colors filled one of the porches. It was a spot of summer beauty in the dead of winter.

I stopped to see what kind of flowers could be growing in winter's cold. To my amazement, I realized they were fake flowers. Baskets and pots overflowing with colorful plastic flowers. Pots and planters of flowers in yellows, reds, pinks, and purples that created an unexpected and joyful display.

I felt my spirits lift seeing those flowers on that gray day. I smiled. Over the course of the winter, I drove by the apartment several times to get a dose of colorful flowers.

At first, I was perplexed by my attraction to the fake flowers, but then realized that it no longer mattered that the flowers were fake. Seeing them lifted my spirits on the grayest of days.

My preconceptions about plastic flowers had prevented me from seeing their potential beauty. Once I changed how I thought about them, I saw how they added beauty.

Continuing this line of thinking, I realized there might be quite a bit of beauty in the world I was missing because of ideas I had about what beautiful is. I decided to try to look at things without applying what I usually thought about them. I started to see beauty in unexpected places.

Instead of seeing a dirty puddle from winter's rain, I saw the reflection of a blue, cloud-filled sky. Instead of seeing a depressing gray landscape of winter, I saw a world at rest. Instead of seeing pointless plastic flowers, I saw beauty.

A few weeks ago when I drove past the apartment, I noticed hummingbird feeders hanging on the porch. I wondered if the colorful plastic flowers would attract hummingbirds sooner than at other places.

94

Within a couple days, I saw the first hummers at my feeders, first attracted by the red gourd hanging on the porch. I bet the little birds had already shown up at the apartment, too, attracted by the red plastic flowers.

Living flowers have returned with springtime, yet I still see the beauty of the plastic flowers when I drive by. But I do not think I would ever feel the same peace surrounded by fake flowers that I do when I sit near my garden surrounded by real flowers.

I feel a connection with the plants each spring as I watch them grow, flower, set seed, and then sleep again. The red rose bush, purple verbena, yellow daylilies, and pink rose campion all seem to exude an energy of peace when I sit by the garden. Plastic flowers just sit there, unchanged by the seasons.

I cannot imagine having plastic flowers, but who knows? There may come a day when I can no longer tend a garden yet still want the beauty of blooming flowers. I may not feel the same connection with plastic flowers, but, now that I no longer view them as pointless, I will enjoy their colors and the beauty they add to the world in their own way.

Especially on gray winter days.

*What little slice of my life would I have missed today
if I had not slowed down?*

Take time to enjoy view
in life's walk

Usually, I spend Monday mornings working on my column. More often than not, I am highly stressed. I agonize over just the right words to use. I think only of creating the best finished product.

This week I did something different. I went for a walk. I haven't walked in a while and wouldn't have this morning if Maia had not suggested it. Because of our walk I scrapped the column I had been working on for this week and wrote this instead.

I enjoyed writing this week. I enjoyed it because I was not thinking about making it the best or thinking about the end product, but because I slowed down enough to enjoy the process.

We had not been walking for long before Maia turned to me and asked, "Are you just walking, or are you enjoying the view?" I was kind of dumbstruck as I pondered her question.

What was I doing? I was not enjoying – or even noticing – the view.

I had set out at a pace to cover the close to 3.2-mile loop in a respectable amount of time. Maia had been pointing out a few things she saw along the way. I just shrugged or said "uh-huh" and kept moving. I didn't want to get slowed down or distracted. I wanted to finish and feel like I had done something.

How many of us approach life that way? I think especially of new graduates who head out to get the right job, a car, a house, and the list goes on. Years roll by, and we may get those things, but what have we missed in the process if we did not slow down to enjoy the journey? To enjoy the view? We miss our lives.

I will tell you what little slice of my life I would have missed today if I had not slowed down.

I would have missed learning about the empty house where Maia and her friends played on the roof when they were young. I would have missed the fields filled with little bright yellow flowers dancing in the breeze. I would have missed the huge black crow that called to us from a yard.

I never would have noticed the yard with many large trees that would be a great place to hang hammocks and have a slumber party with friends. I never would have seen the pretty glassed-in room on the back of one house or the nice cement driveway with no cracks at another.

I had never noticed these things before in my hurry to get the best time and best cardiovascular workout.

I would not have remembered the time Maia kicked a ball out of the fence when she was in elementary school, and we went searching for it when I picked her up. I didn't think we would find it, but she felt bad about losing the ball. We found it a block away at the dry cleaners. I was glad I had taken the time to help her find it.

I never would have seen the house with an unmowed yard full of the little yellow flowers or noticed how it looked like a peaceful Thomas Kincaide painting.

I would not have noticed the nice fenced-in back yard that gives one of the dogs we see plenty of room to run and play. I had seen the dog sitting on a side porch and wondered if it ever got to go out.

I would not have noticed that the mulberry tree where the girls used to collect berries had been cut back so its branches no longer overhung the road.

But most of all I would have missed talking and laughing with my daughter, enjoying the view and the journey and the memories.

I felt better when we finished walking than times when I pushed to go as fast as I could. Taking time to enjoy the view and the journey uplifted my spirits like no amount of exercise could have.

"It is good to have an end to journey toward; but it is the journey that matters, in the end."

– **Ursula K. Le Guin**

Brilliant insights, mental monsters

On July 12, 2001, I stood outside the emergency room at Randolph Hospital sobbing in handcuffs and shackles, the blistering pavement burning through the ugly hospital socks on my feet. I felt humiliated.

I remember the day because it was my mom's birthday. I had overdosed, almost died, and was now waiting to be transported by the sheriff's department to Dorothea Dix Hospital, which was one of our state's mental hospitals.

I was in shackles and cuffs because when I was told I was being involuntarily committed to the state hospital I became very scared and angry and pretty much tore up the intensive care unit room I was in.

I have bipolar illness. I was diagnosed in 1998.

I can only imagine the shock some people may have just felt reading those words. I have a mental illness. It blesses me with brilliant insights while cursing me with all sorts of mental monsters.

People have told me how I seem to see things

that others miss or simply cannot see. They tell me how they are inspired by the things I write about.

I believe I see the world differently because of my mental illness. I have been inspired to use my creativity and use writing to help me make sense of the things I have experienced living with bipolar illness. But I have not written about my mental illness because it is not considered an asset in our world, but rather a liability or something to be feared.

Doctors say mental illness is caused by a chemical imbalance in the brain, no different than diabetes is caused by a chemical imbalance in the pancreas. I use medications and lifestyle changes to manage my illness, just like a diabetic.

People can say, "I have diabetes," and no one bats an eye. But say you have mental illness, and most people get really uncomfortable.

May was Mental Health Awareness month. Every week during May, I felt like I needed to write about my mental illness. I could not. I could not because of "what people might think." Then I realized that if I didn't write about it, people might go on thinking negatively about it, but, just maybe, if I did write about it, there was a chance people might start thinking differently.

Maybe people would start talking about it and sharing personal experiences or the experiences they have had with a family member. Maybe there could be a collective sigh of relief in supporting one another and helping one another.

Maybe. Just maybe. I decided to take the risk.

I have experienced many episodes of mania (having lots of energy) and a couple really bad episodes of depression that lasted about a year. I have been hospitalized many times. In between times, I feel mostly like other people.

I have had times feeling the world is the most beautiful place to live. But I also have had extremely manic episodes when I have behaved in ways I would not usually behave. I have hurt people. I have deep regrets. I have been so depressed I could hardly get out of bed for days.

I have not always taken medications because of side effects, and sometimes because I felt better. Sometimes I seemed to be going along fine then spun into mania again, which is always followed by a depressed period. Because of the uncertainty of my moods, I have isolated over the years.

I have a family and a few close friends who are knowledgeable about mental illness and have always been very supportive, but there have been times when I was so sick it became too much for them to bear. My behavior was so bizarre they simply could not deal with me anymore for a period of time and did not know what to do to help me because I would not listen to anything anyone said.

The very thing that has inspired me to use my creativity has at times nearly destroyed me. Each day I try to use my gift to benefit the world.

Some days I live in fear knowing that no matter what I do, there is always the chance I might become sick again.

I hope that one day we will live in a world where mental illness is not something we fear, but something we recognize as an illness with no stigma attached. Where saying, "I have bipolar illness," will cause no more alarm than saying, "I have diabetes."

Go at your pace
in the race of life

The sign said "Wildlife Crossing" and showed a picture of a rabbit and a turtle. I smiled. Here I was again, jogging at a pace that was not comfortable for me, fighting cramps in my side. I continued like that a little more before I slowed to a walk.

"Go ahead," I told Maia, who reluctantly continued jogging. We had always stayed together during the annual Run Wild 5K at the N.C. Zoo. I had, in years past, been in better shape.

I continued at a fast walk that was more comfortable. This was the fourth year Chip and I had done the race, and the third year Maia participated. It was my first year mostly walking.

I kept jogging slowly, off and on, not feeling that it was quite right to be "just" walking. Even when the hip that I hurt jogging several years ago started bothering me, I felt like I wasn't really doing the race by walking.

Then I thought of the rabbit and the turtle again. So what if the turtle went slowly? It was moving.

It would get where it was going. With that thought, I felt more comfortable. I was moving. I would get where I was going.

In years past, when I jogged and was focused on finishing with the best time, I would get a little annoyed at some of the people who passed me.

I have never been a fast jogger, but I felt like I set a pretty good pace.

Still, people pushing strollers passed me. People who looked like they were not in very good shape passed me. Kids passed me. I would be huffing and puffing and concentrating on just putting one foot in front of the other as people dressed in tutus and animal costumes passed me, talking and laughing.

This year, as I watched people pass, I was not annoyed. I smiled at some of the costumes. I admired parents and children, hand-in-hand, slowly jogging along. I offered encouraging words to some. Some offered encouraging words to me.

Zoo volunteers stood along the paths offering encouragement and making sure participants were OK. Just before I started a long uphill climb, they offered water as we went by. Other years, I kept moving past the water station. But I was thirsty. This year, I took time to drink.

When I got to the downhill part of the race toward the end, I started jogging slowly again. Then I walked for a little bit before slowly jogging across the finish line.

106

Chip and Maia had already finished, pretty close together in time. Chip cheered as I came in, and Maia handed me a bottle of water. We each had gone at our own pace and congratulated each other for a race well done.

As I stood looking at all the people who had finished the race, I thought how different life would be if we all slowed down and approached it more like I had approached this year's Zoo Run.

• Go at your own pace. Be OK with that. Be OK with the pace others go. Don't try to make them go at a pace that is not comfortable for them.

• Watch out for each other and offer encouraging words.

• Celebrate other people's accomplishments – not just winning.

• Take time to drink the water when you are thirsty (eat when you are hungry, rest when you are tired, and so on).

Lastly, and maybe most importantly:

As we were leaving, a kids' run started. Halfway down the parking lot a little girl fell and scraped her knees. She sat there crying and not getting up. Her father, who was carrying a baby, went to her, took her hand, and held it as they walked together to the finish line.

• When someone falls down, sometimes they can get up and go on, but sometimes they can't on their own. Be willing to offer your hand to help someone up and help them finish the race.

*I like being able to find a happy thought
– or a container when I need one.*

Sorting the cabinets
(of my mind) and house

I didn't put my hand up in time as I opened the cabinet. An avalanche of containers spilled out. I stood looking at the mess on the floor. One more container fell out, as if the final big drum roll of some accomplishment.

"Did we get your attention this time?" the containers seemed to ask.

I took a deep breath. The dreaded storage container cabinet. Maybe some people have tidy stacking containers and finding just the right size for leftovers is a breeze. I have seen them advertised on TV. Not me.

I have a few containers from sets that we bought or got at the grocery store with points we earned buying groceries. But most of the containers are from Chinese takeout or containers that once held pimento cheese or egg salad. Then there are the odds and the ends that I do not remember where they came from or what they once contained.

Over the years, I have cleaned the cabinet out a few times. I used to keep glass jars and takeout food boxes, too, but these were never used and just took up space, so I stopped keeping them.

Usually, when the containers fell out, I would stuff all the pieces back in the best way I could and close the door. I still knew that clutter was there, which always left me dreading the next time I needed to open the cabinet.

It was time to do something.

As I sat sorting through containers, I thought about other areas of my life that collected clutter like the cabinet – closets, drawers, trunks of cars.

I thought about my mind. It could get so cluttered with worry and fear thoughts that it was difficult to find and hold onto thoughts of peace and hope and love. I decided to work cleaning out my mental cabinet while I cleaned out the kitchen cabinet.

It is easier to maintain these spaces rather than waiting until they are so cluttered everything falls out onto the floor.

I sorted container bottoms and tops to figure out which ones matched. I had learned that if I stored bottoms stacked in each other and the tops separately, I could fit more containers into the cabinet. But when it came time to get a container it was a real pain trying to find the matching top.

There were several containers with opaque white bottoms and blue tops that I rarely used because you could not see what was in them without taking the lids off. They often would be forgotten

110

in the refrigerator until whatever was in them was no longer edible.

Maybe I didn't need so many containers. Some were not very useful. Just like some of my thoughts. Did I ever use the pie pans I had saved? No. What about the tiny containers big enough for maybe one serving of something? Rarely.

As I discarded containers, I began identifying and discarding negative thoughts.

Bye-bye pie pans and worry thoughts.

Later, odd lids and fear thoughts.

I worked a long time.

When I put the containers I was keeping back into the cabinet, everything stacked neatly, even with lids on. I would be able to find what I needed. The cabinet was a more pleasant place.

I closed the door, then opened it again, and smiled. No longer would I dread opening the cabinet and having something fall out.

The cabinet of my mind felt better too – for a while. Unlike the containers, the negative thoughts I discarded did not want to stay in the trash. I developed awareness of these thoughts though, and I can keep putting them in the trash until they do stay there.

I like being able to find a happy thought when I need one, without having to sort through all sorts of clutter.

Weed vines before they take over your life

I used to like vines. I would search them out and intentionally plant them. "Vine" is now a four-letter word to me. I wish I had never planted a single vine at our house.

Last week, Chip and I worked all week clearing vines and shrubbery that had gotten very overgrown. He took a week of vacation. He's probably glad to be back at work this week so he can rest.

Monday we started with the worst area – trumpet vine that had overgrown a 10-foot-tall trellis and had grown up our house to the peak of the roof. Its vines cascaded down from the edge of the roof and hung outside the bathroom window like some weird plant curtain.

I brought the trumpet vine to our house nearly 20 years ago. I didn't mean to bring that vine though. I had seen a passionflower vine growing in a field beside the house we used to live in near Coleridge. I thought the passionflower was the most beautiful bloom with its delicate tendrils of purples and pinks.

I later returned and dug up a couple of the vines and planted them at our trellis. The next year they nearly covered the trellis and then started blooming orange trumpet-shaped flowers. I decided to leave them because hummingbirds love trumpet vine flowers.

Over the next few years, the vines continued to grow and grow and grow. Some of the vines got to be the size of small tree limbs. They climbed up the house. We cut them down off the house. By the end of the next season, they would be growing up the house again.

Several years passed when we did not get out in the yard to trim the trumpet flower vines or other vines that sprouted around the yard. We did not trim the small trees that volunteered in areas we did not mow. Privet became treelike.

So on Monday when we went out to tackle the trumpet vine, I felt like we would never make any headway and felt like giving up before we even began.

"Just focus on this one area, not all the areas at once," Chip told me. "If you try to look at all of it at once you will get overwhelmed and not be able to do anything."

I took a deep breath, gathered up an armful of vines he had cut, and hauled them to the street. I hauled load after load of vines. I just kept focusing on each armload I carried to the street. It took several hours, but eventually the vines were cut to the ground and hauled to the street.

I looked around the yard at all the other overgrown areas and once again felt paralyzed, not knowing where to start. Chip moved to an area where a pussy willow was overgrown with a very invasive clematis and a wicked vine called green brier that has thorns that will slice you like barbed wire. He started cutting.

He was looking at the next item on the imaginary list, while I looked at the whole list.

The list was overwhelming, but one item could be tackled.

Nearly every day, we worked several hours out in the yard. We cleared areas and could see parts of our yard we had not seen in years. We made breathing space. By the end of the week we had brush piled all the way across our front yard about neck high.

Tackling one item at a time made the work easier, but another thing I realized was that it was a lot easier to maintain things than to let them get overgrown or out of control and then have to do something about them.

It would have been much easier to pull or cut little vines when they first started to grow than to have to do the clearing we had to do.

The same applies to life. It's much easier to address problems as they arise rather than wait until they have grown several seasons and then try to do something about them.

Those vines cascading off the house are something else to contend with.

*Often the new is more wonderful
than you could have imagined.*

Clear out old memories; make room for new

The tree limb lay in an awkward position on the ground, its large, heart-shaped leaves forming a carpet where it had minutes ago formed a shady canopy just above the grass.

I felt a sick, sinking feeling and looked at the catalpa tree trunk again to make sure I wasn't mistaken.

I wasn't mistaken.

The large limb where the girls had once sat and hung upside down was gone, cut away from the tree, forever removed.

I stood there feeling panicked, not knowing what to do or say. Chip had said he was going to cut the limb back. I had agreed. It had gotten so big you couldn't see the rest of the yard or mow under it.

He did a good job, cutting it off in pieces from its end so when he made the final cut at the trunk the weight of the limb would not pull the limb down, possibly injuring the tree.

I still stood silent and shocked.

I could see the part of the limb that was slightly

bent down in a curve where the girls had played for hours. I could see the smoothed-off bark from all the hours where little hands and legs and bodies had crawled on the limb, which was now on the ground.

"It's what needed to be done," I finally told myself.

"You did a really good job cutting back that big limb," I told him, not wanting to ruin the rest of our day working in the yard by getting emotional about the limb.

We worked several more hours, but I could not get the limb off my mind. I kept glancing back over there as if it might magically be re-attached to the tree.

I kept remembering warm summer days when the girls played in the tree and often came to that branch where they could hang upside-down, like on a jungle gym, and then, holding on with their hands, flip off onto the ground. I remembered them sitting on the limb and calling me to bring them something to drink.

With the limb gone, I felt like the memory of that time was leaving me. How many times had I sat on these back steps looking at that limb and remembering those good times?

"That was the limb the girls used to sit on," I finally told him. "I am really feeling sad that it is gone, but the tree looks great, and you did a good job. I'll get over it."

He said he remembered the girls climbing all over the tree, but nothing special about that limb.

Later, when Maia came out to help us haul branches to the street, she commented how we had cut off the limb she used to sit on. She wasn't emotional or upset.

That evening I went out and sat on the steps. I looked where the limb had been and could see only emptiness. I cried. I cried because I felt like that limb connected me to that time and now that it was gone that time would disappear too.

I sat and cried off and on until it started getting dark. As I looked into the empty space, sparkling lights caught my eye. Fireflies filled the backyard creating a magical light show that I had not been able to see all summer because the leaves on the limb blocked the view.

I felt a peace come over me.

The next morning, I went out on the steps and patches of sunlight danced on the ground beneath the tree. I looked up and noticed a large limb that will be perfect for a swing.

I realized that you have to clear out the old to make room for the new to enter, and often the new is more wonderful than you could have imagined.

I had imagined the possibility of grandchildren one day playing on the limb like their mothers had. Instead, there will be a tree to climb and a swing to be pushed in and stories told of the limb where two little girls, now with children of their own, had once climbed.

If we don't have any grandchildren, that will be OK, too. I think Chip and I will be content to push each other in that swing, telling each other stories.

The limb may be gone, but the memories remain.

And new memories will be made.

*If I looked for fun in tasks,
the work would be a lot easier.*

Dreading chores?
It's all about approach

The Bermuda grass had been creeping into the flower bed all summer. I had pulled it up several times. Within days it would be back, poking pointy little tips through the pine needles.

I walked by the flower bed for weeks, watching as the grass crept farther and farther into the flower bed, and tried to pretend I did not see it.

I used to be able to squat and pull weeds for hours. It was meditative and calming.

Not anymore. My legs get tired. My knees hurt. My hips hurt. Weeding now seems more like work than fun.

One day when I walked by the flower bed, I realized if I did not do something the Bermuda grass would soon take over most of the bed. Reluctantly, I got my gloves and knife (to dig out as many roots as I could) and stood by the bed dreading the work ahead. I had to weed by hand because the flowers grow very close together.

I squatted, knowing that within minutes my

knees and hips would be aching. I pulled the long runners until I could tell where they were coming through the pine needles. I ran my hand under the pine needles to pull the runners up and cut as many as I could.

After about 15 minutes, I sat down. It didn't look like I had done anything. I felt tired, and my knees were beginning to ache.

I decided to work another 15 minutes before calling it quits. As I started weeding again, a flash of orange fur flew out from among the flowers and pounced on my hand. Copper, one of our kittens, had seen the movement under the pine needles and decided it was prey.

I petted him for a few minutes then resumed weeding – or trying to weed. Soon his sister joined the action. They both pounced on my hand and each other.

They would attack and then dash behind some flowers to await the next opportunity to spring out and try to catch whatever varmint they thought was moving around in the flower bed. I realized I wasn't going to get much done with them "attacking," so I joined in their play.

I would grab grass, and they would grab my hand. I would wrestle with them until they retreated, then I would get more grass.

I found myself smiling and laughing at their silly kitten antics. Before I knew it almost an hour passed. I had gotten most of the grass out of the bed and had fun doing it. The kittens had captured many pretend critters.

I squatted the whole time, yet my knees and hips didn't ache, and I didn't feel too tired. It had felt like I was playing rather than working.

Dreading work made me ache. Approaching it playfully made me feel good. I decided to approach other work with a playful spirit.

I needed to water several trees in pots. I had to untangle the hose but made it a game, and it wasn't bad at all. As I moved the stream of water from one pot to another, a dragonfly hovered near one of the pots. Usually, I would have ignored it and kept on watering. Instead I turned the hose skyward. The dragonfly skipped and danced through the water falling down like summer rain.

As I watched its graceful flight, I noticed rainbows in the water droplets. We played like this for several minutes, the dragonfly and me. I held the hose overhead and let the water fall on me, imagining rainbows cascading down over my head.

I felt "happy" course through my body. I smiled.

And you know what? I could have sworn that the dragonfly and the trees were smiling, too.

Don't let 'spider webs' stall your 'nest-building'

I have been watching a paper wasp build its nest on our front porch for several weeks. It is building in a corner of the far end of the porch where it will not bother anyone, so I am letting it build.

Only thing is, it appears to have stopped building.

At first, it seemed to be busy all day coming and going and adding more cells where it would eventually lay eggs. But in the past week, the work has stopped. The wasp just sits there most of the day. I have not seen it come and go for days.

It was a couple weeks ago when a house spider started building a web under the paper wasp's nest. As the web got bigger and messier each day, it created an obstacle course for the wasp to navigate when flying in and out of its nest.

It seems the wasp has tired of contending with the web and has given up.

I have seen many paper wasp nests over the years under the edges of the house and in trees.

Some have been the size of basketballs. The wasps have always seemed undaunted by anything when nest-building.

I am perplexed as to why the wasp has allowed a spider's web to prevent it from doing the work it set out to do.

One day as I watched the spider spin its web and the wasp sit there, I started thinking about how I have allowed "spider webs" in my life prevent me from doing things.

The spider kept weaving, side to side. I thought about how each strand could represent something that had happened in my life that made me start acting differently. Things that made me forget what it was I came here to accomplish in the first place. Things that made me stop and sit still on my nest.

The wasp started out knowing its mission was to build a nest, lay eggs, and protect them. We start out full of love and promise and hope. We want to make a positive difference in the world.

Then the spiders in our lives get busy, stringing webs around us. They weave mental strands of fear, loneliness, mistrust, betrayal, self-doubt, and hopelessness that can stop us in our tracks.

I want to tell the wasp there are going to be things that happen in life that can wear a body out if we sit back and do nothing about them.

I want to tell that wasp to remember who it came here to be. To fly through that web – because it

126

could if it tried. I want to tell that wasp not to give up. Rest, if necessary, but do not give up.

I want to tear down the spider web, so the wasp can get back to doing what it started out doing.

But I won't. The wasp is going to have to break through the web. Just like we are the only ones who can break through webs that ensnare us at times.

I will watch the story unfold and try to give myself the same encouragement I want to give the wasp, so I can begin dismantling webs I have allowed to be built around me.

Maybe as I make progress on this front, the wasp will free itself from the web that surrounds it, too. I hope so.

*When you encounter a person – or wild plant –
you never know what beauty they may one day produce.*

Give weeds a chance
– and time to bloom

I am a grower of weeds. Very little growing in my yard any more is intentional, although at one time it was. Even then, my plants looked like weeds to people who didn't know what they were.

Years ago, my brother surprised me and cut the grass while I was not home. It was nice to come home and find the grass had been cut.

Later that evening when I walked through the yard, I realized several of my "weeds," which were unusual herbs, had been mowed also. I didn't mind. I knew they would grow back. I was grateful he had mowed the grass.

Every year, our front walk is an experiment of sorts, with odd plants growing here and there until I determine if they are some sort of flowering plant or, well, just a weed.

One year a particularly unusual plant sprouted in the walkway. I watched as it started forming a bulbous green growth on a long, slender stalk. Within a few days, I went out one morning to find a flower of fiery red petals with a deep-purple-and-black center. When I looked it up, I discovered that it was a poppy.

I have no idea where the poppy came from, but for several days we were in awe of it. It seemed to glow as it grew in the walkway. And to think I might have yanked it up as a weed!

A couple of years ago, a man confused my front flowerbed as an overgrown part of the yard that needed to be mowed. The bed used to be home to coneflowers, daisies, and phlox, but over the years most of these died out.

I stopped watering the bed when I realized I could not provide enough water to do anything other than keep the flowers hanging on during times of drought. I decided just to see what plants could survive.

The bed has since been overtaken by a flower I do not know that usually blooms an almost florescent yellow around mid-July. Until they bloom, the plants look like tall bunches of weeds.

This year, the bunches of greenery grew extra tall, some standing chest high. By mid-July there were no signs of buds that would produce flowers. I thought maybe I had just let some odd plant grow and that these plants weren't the ones that had produced the yellow flowers for years.

It was so hot and dry the plants wilted nearly every day and then rebounded overnight. I watered them once to see if they would form

130

flowers. By the end of July, there were still no flowers.

Finally, early in August, we got some really good rain. Within a few days, buds started appearing and, within a week, the small bright yellow flowers began opening. The flower bed no longer looked like a mess of weeds.

The flowers, a little larger than a silver dollar, are formed from eight yellow petals around a round brown center. Even though small, they were so profuse they formed a bright yellow blanket that swayed in the breeze.

As I watched butterflies and goldfinches visit the flowers, I thought about how people can be like these flowers, not "blooming" for the longest time. They could be mistaken for "weeds." But the right rain or thoughtful deed or kind word can be just what flowers – and people – need to bloom.

I enjoy the plants I planted that have survived over the years. But I always get excited each new spring at the "weeds" that appear in my garden and walkway.

You never know when you encounter a wild plant what beauty it might one day produce if you don't write it off as a "weed."

When possible, we probably are better off singing and dancing through difficult times.

Facing the 'traffic jams' in life

Brake lights lit up on cars ahead of us as we traveled down Interstate 85 at close to 70 miles per hour. Within seconds, traffic was slowing to 40, 30, 20 mph and then a crawl before coming to a standstill.

We had not left with much extra time to encounter a delay and still get our daughter to the RDU Airport in time to catch her flight. I wondered why we had stopped.

As traffic slowed, I noticed the people in vehicles next to us. Many were looking at their cell phones. I wondered if they were checking email or trying to find out what was up ahead. Maybe they were trying to find alternate routes to where they were going. Many looked annoyed.

As we started moving very slowly, a car pulled alongside with a driver who seemed to be enjoying the ride. He "danced" in his seat and appearing to be singing along with his radio. He turned to me and smiled.

He seemed undisturbed by the delay, accepting

that it was just part of life.

Once we got through whatever was slowing us down, he likely would continue with his day in a good frame of mind, unlike many of the travelers who looked super-stressed out.

I noticed many vehicles getting off at exits. Maybe they had found an alternate route around the traffic jam. They might be bound for side roads, then come back onto the interstate miles ahead and avoid the stop-and-go traffic.

I wondered if we should try to get off the interstate, too. But who's to say that there wouldn't be things to slow the travelers who chose to take an alternate route? I wondered what lay ahead. How long would this slow crawl last? If we had known there would be a delay, we would have left earlier.

None of us had left our homes that morning anticipating delays in getting to where we were going. None of us knew what had caused the delay. We were simply stuck and had to trust that eventually everything would begin moving as it should.

As we idled along, I thought how life is sometimes just like that. We can be motoring along at 70 mph with no problems when, out of nowhere, something happens that slows or stops us in our tracks.

Do we fight against the events causing delay, try a detour, or do we sing and dance our way through, learning what we can from the experience?

I thought about another time, when I was coming home from the same airport after dark and a heavy snow blanketed the interstate in minutes. I was terrified and afraid I would be stranded on the side of the road. I was not singing and dancing. I was barely creeping down the highway.

Just when I felt I could no longer plow through the snow, an 18-wheeler pulled around me. I drove in its tracks, following it off the interstate to a truck stop with a restaurant, where I stayed overnight. I vowed to keep a blanket in my car during in winter in case I was ever stranded.

On this trip with our daughter, there was no snow, of course. Finally, we came up to two cars pulled to the side of the highway – the vehicles damaged, but the occupants apparently OK. After we passed, traffic began moving at normal speed again. We made it to the airport in time.

We will encounter "traffic jams" in life. We need to have faith we will make it through OK and try to remember that when the going gets tough, we can often find help – like the tractor-trailer rig on that snowy night.

When possible – and it's not always possible – we probably will find we are better off singing and dancing through difficult times instead of fretting or fighting.

Sometimes you have to try many different ways before you get it right.

Life comes without directions; keep trying

The wallpaper would not stick to the wall. No matter what we tried, after a few minutes, it started sliding down or peeling off the wall.

Mom and I had hung a lot of wallpaper. The whole house was wallpapered except the dining room, which we decided to tackle several years ago. To start, we had hung a heavy paper over the paneled walls so when we put up the decorative wallpaper the crevices between panels would be covered.

The paper we were trying to hang was not pre-pasted like all the paper we had hung before. As each piece slid off the wall, we laid it out again and applied even more water trying to better activate the paste and make the paper stick. The paper would not stick.

After an hour or so, we decided to look at the directions.

Once we mixed paste and then applied it to the paper, it clung to the wall like it was supposed to.

It's good to read directions.

They can help you figure out how to do things you do not know how to do. But sometimes directions only give possibilities for resolving whatever you are tackling.

It is not always as clear-cut as simply applying the paste to the paper.

I read lots of books when I was pregnant to learn about pregnancy. When I had a baby, I read lots of books about babies to learn what to do. There were many suggestions for dealing with various situations.

Some worked. Some didn't. We tried many things until we found just what helped soothe our colicky baby and how to relieve teething pain.

When I began gardening, I read lots of books to learn how to garden. Again, there were many different directions for growing the biggest tomatoes, keeping squash bugs from decimating squash, stopping pepper blossoms from falling off before they set fruit.

Some worked. Some didn't. I tried different approaches year after year until something worked.

You can't just give up in the middle of rearing children or growing gardens. You have to keep working to find an answer for whatever is going on. Resolving problems dealing with living things is not as simple as dealing with wallpaper.

Right now I feel like throwing my hands in the

air and giving up. I am going through medication changes to help me with bipolar illness. The medications I took for many years seem to have stopped working like they should.

Getting the right medications to help with any illness can be frustrating, whether it's diabetes, high blood pressure, or a mental illness. Sure, there are directions that tell what each medication should do, but each of us is different, and our bodies react differently to medications.

Right now it pretty much feels like my wallpaper is not sticking very well to the wall. I wish I could just follow directions, apply some paste, and have the problem resolved. I have little patience for allowing my body to adjust to a new medication. I want it to work now. I want to feel better now.

Over the weekend when I talked to my mom about how difficult it was going through yet another medication change, she reminded me to give myself a break. To relax and not be so hard on myself. To remember that such things take time – just like rearing children or growing a garden.

Sometimes you have to try many different ways before you get it right.

I have found when going through difficult times a sense of humor can help tremendously. I remember a funny card I saw years ago. It said: "This is a test. This is only a test. If this was your actual life you would have been given better instructions."

Getting to know those 'nasty old possums'

I thought I knew possums. Yes, possums. Growing up I never heard them called opossoms. Just plain ol' possum.

I never saw a possum in the neighborhood where I grew up. I guess there were not enough woods, or they kept to themselves.

But I knew about them. They didn't seem to be very smart. I saw a lot of them dead on the roads. I heard many times, "There's another nasty old possum," when we drove by a carcass.

So that's what they were to me – nasty old possums.

Even during the few years we lived in the country before we bought a house on the edge of Ramseur, I never once saw a live possum. It wasn't until we had lived in Ramseur a few years that I had my first personal encounter.

We had nine or 10 cats then who mostly lived outdoors. They ate in a shed behind our house. We put a cat door in the door on the shed to give them a sheltered place to eat and sleep at night. All the cats figured out how to go in and out the door. What we didn't realize is that other animals had also learned to use the cat door.

One night I heard a terrible fight in the shed. It sounded like several animals were killing each other. I wasn't sure that the sounds I heard were cats.

I was afraid to open the shed door and see what was going on, so I threw a flower pot at the side of the building. The commotion stopped for a few seconds before a huge possum stuck its head out the cat door, hissed at me, and retreated inside to start the brawl again.

I didn't know what to do. I was certain one or more of our cats was in there getting mauled. It took a while to get the situation under control, but when all was said and done, it turned out the possum had been fighting with a raccoon.

For many years after that, possums weren't just nasty things to me, they were mean and vicious creatures, too.

Many years later, I volunteered at a wildlife rescue. One of the permanent residents was a possum. When I saw it, I wondered why anyone would ever keep a possum.

After several weeks of watching it, I realized that it seemed quite peaceful. I eventually fed it and petted it. Its fur was silky soft, and it seemed to like being petted. I read articles about possums and learned they are marsupials and that they carry their young in a pouch.

My opinion of possums changed. I felt intrigued rather than revolted. I learned how smart they are, too, and the reason behind the saying "playing possum."

I stopped once to move a possum that appeared to have been hit by a car out of the road. It looked dead, but I couldn't see any injuries as I placed it on the side of the road. As I drove away, I looked in my rearview mirror and saw it get up and walk into the woods.

I thought I knew possums, but I did not. I based my opinions on what other people told me and on a single encounter. I am glad I had the opportunity to get to know them better and let them become one of my "friend" wild animals.

Often when I sit on the front porch at night before bedtime, with the porch light off, listening to the crickets, a possum will climb onto the chest at the end of the porch where we now feed our cats.

It is nice to welcome its arrival rather than feel fearful and angry. It will look at me sitting in the chair and then settle in and eat cat food before rambling off.

I am glad I am at peace with possums. It is much better than being at odds with them.

We need to get past seeing differences with our eyes.

To the 'teachers' and a lesson on crowds

I watched as the man with the white-tipped cane navigated the street. Sliding the stick along in front of him, he walked around trash cans, tent poles, and people along South Fayetteville Street during the annual fall festival.

He stopped every now and then and seemed perfectly at ease in the crowd. I was not. Crowds of people have always made me very uncomfortable.

I watched from our vendor's tent for nearly an hour as he made his way up and down the street. I wanted to speak to him, but I did not know what to say. I did not approach him.

I realized he "saw" the world differently from everyone around him. He likely noticed sounds, smells and the way the environment "felt" more than those of us who relied mainly on seeing things. He didn't see the differences I saw that made me not approach people, that made me feel uncomfortable in crowds.

I decided to listen to the crowd like him rather

145

than look at it. I closed my eyes and listened. At first, the crowd noise was a pleasant humming sound. Then I noticed individual sounds within the hum – people talking and laughing, friendly people making happy sounds. I felt at ease.

I opened my eyes, saw the throng of people, and felt uneasy. I closed my eyes and listened again.

I heard babies crying. It sounded like there were many babies crying. When I opened my eyes, I expected to see crying babies everywhere. I saw one.

Then I imagined all the people as the babies they once had been. When I looked at them that way, our differences disappeared. I felt a kinship.

We all were babies once, without fears and judgments. We grew up, and things happened to make us feel separate and different from each other.

I looked around for the man with the cane to go talk with him, but he was gone.

As the weekend rolled on, several other "teachers" helped me feel more comfortable in the crowd.

There were three little girls who skipped along holding hands. Suddenly one yelled "fire" and stopped the other two before they skipped right into a grill where food was being cooked.

A boy stepped into our space and started talking to me about a wind chime we had hanging on our tent. He asked all kinds of questions as if he had known me all his life.

An old friend from junior high stopped by to say "hello" and tell me how he got inspiration from some of the stuff I wrote. He told me he had battled with substance abuse problems but was doing well now.

It took a lot of courage to approach someone he had not seen in more than 30 years and talk candidly about his life. He helped me remember who I had been then. I had not been uneasy in crowds back then.

When it came time to take our tent down, I was having problems. A woman appeared out of nowhere and before I knew it, she had all the poles down, the canvas top off, and all of it packed in its carrying case.

If I see the man with the cane again, I will speak to him. I will tell him how trying to experience the world as I imagined he experienced it helped me remember we are not all so different. That we need to get past seeing differences with our eyes and reach out to each other with our hearts.

I will tell him how he reminded me of something I had read in "All I Really Need To Know I Learned In Kindergarten," a book by Robert Fulghum, which I thought was the best advice I had ever heard for living together in this world: "When you go out into the world, watch out for traffic, hold hands, and stick together."

I have always experienced the Creator most closely in a garden.

When in stress,
stop and smell the soil

The smell of the soil soothed my soul. I had been restless all day, and no amount of anything else had helped.

I sat on the porch all morning thinking and praying. First, I was in the shade, but I sat there so long the sun moved across the sky to shine on me and illuminate the prisms hanging on the porch.

Little rainbows danced around the porch. I hardly noticed.

I tried aromatherapy, but the usually relaxing smell of lavender did not help. I took a nap and awoke still feeling restless.

Our Mama Cat had been hit by a car and killed.

When I headed out for a full day Friday, I was running a little behind. As I got ready to pull onto the highway near our house, I saw her lying beside the highway not far from our street.

I had to go. All I could do was go back to the house and tell our daughter Maia. I hated to leave her with the task of collecting our cat. I had done it once before for another cat, and it was awful.

A kind man stopped and helped Maia collect Mama Cat. That had been divine intervention.

We buried Mama in front of the little pond in our front yard where she had hunted frogs and played with her kittens. As we placed the rock atop her grave, I thought I would feel better, but I was still thinking, thinking, thinking.

I thought about how she would sit by the pond and watch her kittens climbing the cedars nearby and call for them to come down. How she watched them catch butterflies on the butterfly bush. How she once drug one of the kittens out of the street by the scruff of its neck.

Why had she tried to cross the highway? We had her spayed, and I thought she would settle down and live a long and happy life at our house with two of her kittens that we kept from her litter. I imagined a happy little cat family frolicking in the front garden for years.

Their father was a handsome stray – solid white with a black tail – that we had neutered. He had wandered all his life, I suppose, and after he was neutered, he still wandered, coming to visit our house every few days.

Why had I thought having Mama spayed would keep her at our house? She had been a wandering stray before she had her kittens on our front porch.

"Why? Why? Why?" my mind kept asking. I sat down on our front walk to pull weeds and think, still trying to figure this all out with my head.

150

I pulled one weed and then another. I really wasn't thinking about weeding the walkway. It had gotten so bad earlier in the summer I had mowed it. I was just smelling soil. Each time I breathed in, I felt more at peace. My mind stilled.

I watched the black-and-yellow centipedes uncurl and crawl away as I uncovered them. I helped several earthworms into the flower bed. I watched tiny snails slide across the rock border. I saw black four-o'clock seeds in the soil, ready to produce plants in the spring.

I don't know how long I was out there. As dusk set in, I found myself at the end of the walkway, the whole thing weeded. I felt peaceful.

The smell of the soil reminded me that living and dying are natural parts of our existence. People and pets and plants die.

We have seasons of our lives that change from spring to summer to fall to winter. There is a time and purpose to all things.

I have always experienced the Creator most closely in a garden, and once again nature proved to be a valuable teacher.

As I went back up the walkway, I thought about something a woman told me last week. She said her granddaddy always told her, "As long as you're breathing, you will have challenges, concerns, stress. Pray and roll through it."

Yes, pray and roll through it – and remember to stop and smell the soil.

Don't let the 'black dot' become your focus

The privet had gotten so overgrown it was more like a clump of little trees than a bush. So, when we decided to cut it down, we used a saw. It only took a few minutes, and the privet lay on the ground.

Within minutes, I noticed two cardinals – a male and a female – flying frantically around where we had cut the privet. I walked over to see what was upsetting them.

In the middle of the limbs lay a nest with three eggs in it. My heart sank. We had not even thought about inspecting the privet for nests before we cut it. Now it was too late.

The only thing I knew to do was to gather up the nest and nestle it onto a tree limb nearby, hoping the birds would find it.

I watched for nearly an hour as the birds kept flying to the ground where the nest had been and then up into a nearby tree. Finally, the female flew to the limb where I had placed the nest and found it. She flew away. Then both cardinals checked out the nest several times before flying away. They never returned.

I thought about how the birds had worked so hard to build the nest, bringing branch after branch they had gathered from the yard. They had brought vines and small leaves to make the inside of the nest soft and cozy. I imagined how happy they were when the female laid her eggs.

Then all of it was destroyed in a few minutes.

The thing about the birds was that they did not keep coming back to the fallen nest for very long. They were obviously upset by what had happened, but then they flew away. They moved on.

I imagined they were the cardinals I saw later with a new nest in cypress trees on the other side of the yard.

All of this made me think of a story I had read.

A professor passed out a surprise test to his students. The tests were face down. The students were told to turn the paper over and describe what they saw.

There was a black dot in the middle of the page.

When the professor collected the tests, every student had described the black dot – its size and its location on the paper, but no one had mentioned the white space surrounding the dot.

The professor told the students that the small black dot represented the things that happen in our lives that trouble us. The white space around the dot represented the good things in our lives.

We all have many things for which to be grateful, but often we focus on the troubling thing (or things) – the black dot – just as the students did. We do not take our eyes off the dot to see all the good that surrounds us.

The cardinals had focused on the black dot briefly but then saw the white space, the possibilities that existed in the wake of their nest's destruction.

We build up beautiful ideals of how we hope life and people will be. If our ideals are shattered – or even if reality simply falls short of our dreams – we often sit amidst the rubble unable to see the love that surrounds us. Sometimes we get stuck, immobilized by what looks like the utter destruction of our lives.

What if we saw the white space and recognized that the black dot is only a very small part of it all?

Then we could relish every moment we have to build new nests, cherish every moment with loved ones, and see the beauty and love that was there all along.

How lovely it is to let dead things go
to make room for the new to grow.

Be like a tree;
let go of 'dead things'

The leaves cascading from the maple trees pitter-pattered down like a spring shower. The trees seemed to heave a sigh of relief and let go of nearly all their leaves in a matter of minutes, covering the ground in a glowing carpet of yellow.

As I watched, I thought about a sign I recently saw that said: "The trees are about to show us how lovely it is to let the dead things go."

How effortlessly the trees let their leaves go, soon standing there nearly stark naked, making bare-branch silhouettes against the sun.

Not long ago, I began trying to let the "dead things" go after I saw a cartoon where a woman was practicing the Japanese art of de-cluttering. The idea is that you hold an object and if it doesn't bring you joy, you get rid of it. So far, she had gotten rid of her stove and some other things I do not remember.

I started small. A table in our hall that used to serve as a nature table — a place where we brought in neat things we found outside — had become a repository for all sorts of stuff that had become a dust-covered pile.

After studying the items on the table, I selected seven items to keep — three candleholders, a box of incense, an incense burner, and two geodes. I got a bag and out went the dirt dauber nest, the paper wasp nest and the feathers it held, the acorn caps, and various nubs of burnt candles and broken things.

I put the bag on the dining room table to check again before I threw it away. The next day I realized I just needed to take it out to the trash. Which I did. I thought about that bag several times but did not retrieve it.

I cleaned and re-placed the items I had kept for the table, put fresh candles in the holders, and lit them. I asked several people to look at the table. They agreed was much nicer than the previous mess and made them feel peaceful.

I asked them to look at the top of a cabinet in the den that was covered in a mishmash of abandoned items. That cabinet did not convey a feeling of peace.

I wish I could say that I got inspired and went through the house discarding items that no longer brought joy, letting go of these "dead things" as effortlessly as the trees let go of their leaves. I didn't.

I still have not tackled the den cabinet, but over a

couple weeks I have discarded a few other items.

Out went a can of organic cocoa that was several years outdated that I never used. I kept it because it cost so much, but every time I saw it, I felt sad I had never used it. It no longer haunts me from the back of the pantry.

Out went a purple braided cord I made during a low period in my life that lengthened the pull chain on a ceiling fan. It reminded me of that time. I haven't thought about those dark days since it's been gone.

I chucked a little plastic tree covered in white Christmas lights that used to remind me of the spirit of Christmas. The lights no longer worked. It no longer reminded me of the spirit of Christmas.

The dead things we need to jettison may be tangible items, relationships, or ways of thinking that keep you stuck. Letting them go makes space for peace – and new things – to enter.

The trees know. Think about it. What if the trees were so attached to their leaves, they refused to let them fall when the time came? What if they stood covered in dead leaves all winter, and new leaves couldn't grow in the spring? What a mess.

Thank you, trees, for showing how lovely it is to let the dead things go to make room for the new to grow. To make room for the tender green leaves of spring that offer the promise of another season of new life.

*Given time, even broken things can morph
into beautiful works of art.*

Finding the purpose
in every (broken) thing

Sometimes things get broken, by accident or on purpose, and sometimes just by time's passage.

Hearts get broken. Souls get broken. Spirits get broken. Plates, cups, saucers, vases – all get broken.

Broken does not mean useless. Broken just means a thing has taken a different form.

I always think of the line in Leonard Cohen's "Anthem" when I encounter something broken – whether it is an object or a person or an animal: "There is a crack, a crack in everything … that's how the light gets in."

A pottery lighthouse broken to pieces sits on the dining room table, waiting to be repaired to again offer its light to the world. I do not know if I will be able to reconstruct it. Our cat Bella knocked it off a mantel.

Chip has had the lighthouse for as long as I have known him. When we were first married, I loved turning it on as the light faded on early winter nights. I had been caring all day for my first baby and eight orphaned puppies I bottle fed in a shed behind our house. I was tired.

When I turned the lighthouse on, I felt I could make it just a little longer until Chip came pulling in the long dirt drive to our house out in the middle of nowhere near Coleridge.

I understood the hope our seashore's lighthouses give sailors at sea.

I will work on it until it is either put back together, or I realize it is beyond my abilities to repair.

Sometimes we cannot repair broken things. Pieces are missing. Parts are so shattered there is no putting them back together to resemble their former self.

Sometimes we need to call a professional – like for plumbing problems or car problems or people problems. Regardless of our fix-it skills, we may not have the know-how.

I will work on the lighthouse but not too long. I spent two days earlier this year trying to fix a ceramic basket vase that belonged to my grandmother Ruth Esther Snitker Meier. It got broken last year when I carelessly threw a black trash bag full of possessions into a closet.

When I sat down to repair it, pieces of its handle were missing. But it was covered in roses and reminded me of her. It was the last thing I had of hers.

I tried all kinds of glues. I used clothespins and vice grips and books to try to prop it up. Nothing worked. In frustration I finally put all the pieces in a plastic bag and sent it out with the trash.

Looking back, I wish I had saved the pieces. I could have put them in the garden like I did a broken blue pot covered in yellow tulips my mom gave me for my birthday the year after my dad died. I had a peace plant in it. The pot broke, but I still have the plant. No longer useful to hold a plant, it now makes nice hiding places for toads in the summer and mice in the winter.

The chair where I nursed Cally! for endless hours eventually got moved into the back yard for the dogs and then this year got put in the trash pile. Its back was gone, and one leg bent at an odd angle. One day I looked at the chair and saw a table. I pulled it from the trash pile and placed it under the magnolia tree we planted for Maia's birth that now towers as high as our house.

I pulled two old wooden straight-back chairs from the pile and now have a little secret garden spot to sit some days and watch the garden sleeping in winter and dancing during the summer. I have watched sensual fiery sunsets and magical moon risings from under the tree.

I don't know if the lighthouse will ever be returned to its former glory, but I will not throw away its pieces if it cannot be reconstructed as it once was. I will allow it to sit on the dining room table until I can see what it might become. Hands off. Someone bigger than me in charge of its fate.

Every thing has a purpose.

It may not be what it initially appeared to be. Given time even broken things can morph into more beautiful works of art – and let in even more light because they are broken.

With time, healing comes, as do opportunities for new growth.

Storms bring havoc
... and rebirth

The storm came out of nowhere. It came fast. It wreaked destruction unlike any other storm we had experienced in the almost eight years we had lived in our house.

It left trees twisted, branches and leaves slung helter-skelter over the lawn and up onto the porch, and us shaken at how quickly our world can change.

The day had started out like any other. It was sunny and humid, as summers typically are. Chip and I had headed out to work for the U.S. Census Bureau, leaving our two young daughters in the care of a neighborhood friend at our house.

By mid-afternoon, it was sweltering. The heat hung in waves across the roads and haze in the distance. As I headed into a neighborhood in Liberty, where I would be working for several hours, I noticed black clouds to the south, the direction of home.

Within 10 minutes, the babysitter called, terrified by the storm that was raging. I tried to reassure her that it would probably blow out as quickly as it blew in. She said the two maple trees in the front yard appeared to be twisting.

I told her I would be there soon. As I got off the phone, all horror broke loose in Liberty. The sky darkened to what seemed like night, the winds hurled sheets of rain against the side of the house where I was. Marble-sized hail bounced off everything outside.

I realized I would not be able to leave. I tried to call the landline at the house but got no answer. I tried to get Chip on his cell phone. I got no answer. I squashed back the panic I was feeling as the storm raged outside.

After about 15 minutes, the storm subsided enough for me to get in my car and head home. It seemed to take forever.

When I pulled onto our street, several utility company vehicles blocked the way. I stopped behind them and got out. When I looked down the street, I saw the twisted and mangled remains of our maple trees blocking the street. The power lines and phone lines were tangled in their mess.

I ran through front yards to our house, where I found two very frightened little girls and a babysitter on the front porch.

We had spent many summer days in the shade of those two trees reading books and doing art. Tears streaked the faces of the girls and ran down my face as I realized that part of our lives together

166

was gone.

It took the utility crews all afternoon and until close to dusk to clear the debris and cut the two trees down to stumps. It took us days to pile all the rubble beside the street. I could not bring myself to pile the pieces of the trunks at the street. They sat in the yard for a long time.

Weeks after the destruction of our cherished trees, after many tears and asking "why?" far too many times, I ventured into the yard and arranged the stumps into a circle. I worked up the soil inside the circle of our fallen trees and planted tulip bulbs.

The next spring a beautiful bed of tulips filled the area where one tree had stood. We added bulbs year after year, until the stumps rotted away, and squirrels carried off most of the bulbs. We enjoyed the tulips for years.

Storms, in nature and in life, often come unexpectedly and can lay waste to landscapes and lives. But with time, healing comes, as do opportunities for new growth. It may take quite some time to clear away the rubble, but it can be done.

The destruction of the trees seemed like the end, but it was only a new beginning. If the trees had not been destroyed, we never would have known the tulips.

Sometimes when we crash, we can be so stunned
by what happened we lose our bearings and flounder.

Listen for guidance
in the midst of turmoil

I stood watching the reflections of the clouds in the puddle, comparing their shapes in the sky to their shapes in the water. I had gotten into somewhat of a hypnotic state when …

SMACK!!!

… a flying insect pinged me right on the bridge of the nose and crashed into the puddle.

I looked at the insect floundering in the water, possibly wondering how in the world it had gone from full flight to floating.

It appeared to be some sort of flying ant. I watched as it did its best to paddle around the puddle, edging near the sides then turning and heading back toward the middle. It seemed to have lost its bearings not being in flight.

As the ant moved in the water, it disturbed the calm surface, making the cloud reflections morph into shapes very different from their shapes in the sky.

An elephant cloud looked like a dragon in the puddle; a flower appeared to be a bird getting ready to fly.

I realized that the things we see reflected back at us may not always be a true representation of what they are. Reflections can be faulty. Things can appear to be something they are not.

Our thoughts can be like the ant in the puddle, changing the world reflected in our mind to something different than what the world actually is.

I thought I had learned what I needed to know from the ant, and was preparing to rescue it from the puddle, when another ant came walking up to the edge of the puddle.

It could not see the reflections I could see in the puddle. It was not distracted by images that were being affected by the ant disturbing the water's surface. All it seemed to be aware of was the floundering ant.

As I watched, the ant on the edge of the puddle began walking back and forth along the puddle's edge. The ant in the puddle stopped floundering and headed in the direction of the ant on the edge.

Before long the ant that had crashed climbed onto dry ground where its fellow ant stood. The ants checked each other out, then headed off in the same direction.

I realized the real lesson here was that sometimes when we are halted mid-flight and crash into a puddle, we can be so focused and stunned by what happened that we lose bearings

170

and flounder about.

If we can take a moment to look around and listen for guidance, we may just find there is someone – an ant on the edge of the puddle, a fellow traveler, or our Creator – offering encouragement and guidance to find our way.

In your account, you want more days well-lived
than days you struggle to survive.

Keep tabs on your
Bank of Life

What is the average life span for an American these days? 70 years? 25,550 days.

We live in the land of plenty. Of plentiful resources. Of clean water. Yet, many people are Unhappy. Unbalanced. Distressed.

Suicide has become one of our national epidemics. Along with opioid abuse. Obesity. Autoimmune diseases. Depression.

What gives?

When my dad died, he had amassed a considerable amount of money to live comfortably after he retired. He and my mom had 10-12 weeks of timeshares where they would be able to travel all over the world. They had rental property. IRAs. Savings. Investments.

He started out "poor" up at the end of Sheffield Street in Asheboro. Up on Oakie Mountain. He and his parents, sister, and brothers lived there in a four-room house with one bath.

My grandfather Arthur Jordan was a prison

guard who drank and gambled. A jovial man who made life hard for his family because of his habits. He made my life happy when I would cuddle up in his lap in his vinyl-covered recliner. He died when I was five.

My grandmother Beulah Jordan knew how to make a Sunday meal (the big meal of the week eaten after church) with only canned food and maybe a chicken if times were good.

My dad worked hard his whole life. He enlisted in the U.S. Navy and then was able to go to UNC-Chapel Hill through a military program. He was the first male to graduate from the physical therapy program. He worked as a physical therapist at Randolph Hospital until he began doing contract work with agencies in the 1980s.

He made good financially and, in his later days, I believe had a pretty healthy "Bank of Life."

What's a Bank of Life? The days you accumulate that you count as "good" days. Those days that fill your being with joy and peace and comfort. Those days that you have when it is not hard to take a deep breath and your bones don't ache and your being is not worn out, ragged, rubbed thin, and exhausted.

A young person I had just met told me about the Bank of Life. He explained it this way:

You put good days into your Bank of Life account and at the end of those days your life has been well-lived if the number of days in your Bank

174

of Life outnumber the number of days in your bank of "what you had to do to survive in the world."

Say you go out and enjoy walking your dog, or cooking a meal with your partner, or walking in nature, or playing games with friends, or enjoying tea at a nice tea shop ... these days go into your Bank of Life.

And it is this fortune that determines the quality of the life you lived – not all the tangible stuff of the world. Especially not money.

Looking back over my life I think of all the long summer days spent playing until the streetlights came on (which is when I was required to be home) in the woods near our home with my dog Friskie. Those days went into my bank of life.

The days I decided to stay in the woods after dark and try to sneak in through the basement ... not so much. Dad made us pick our own switch off the dogwood tree and if it wasn't big enough he'd make me (or my brother) go back and get a bigger one.

Losing myself in art and gardening and writing until the world around me falls away, and it is just me at one with whatever I am working on, balancing that tiny crystalline castle on the tip of my finger until I can give it the form that flows through me divinely inspired from our Creator – those are Bank of Life moments.

Watching seeds I gently placed in soil sprout and

grow or eating warm tomatoes straight from the garden. Bank of Life moments.

Catching lightning bugs and making glow jars, swimming at Faith Rock in Deep River with a beaver, catching clouds in jars, rolling down grassy slopes in old metal trashcans, catching crawdads in the creek, painting myself brown with creek mud, swinging on rope swings … the feeling of first love … giving birth to my daughters …

All these and so many more are in my Bank of Life. These are the things I try to focus on when the Night Terrors come.

I think I already have more in my Bank of Life than in the bank of the expectations of the world.

Maybe that's why they say I'm CrAzY…

I hope the day never comes when I no longer see the divine spark in every living creature.

If helping others is crazy, call me crazy

The man pushed the shopping cart as fast as he could down N.C. 42 in front of the YMCA, looking over his shoulder for cars coming up behind him.

He pushed the cart off the road for oncoming traffic to pass before he took to the highway again, making it a few more feet before he had to stop again for approaching vehicles.

I saw him as I crested the hill from the opposite direction. I was warm and dry inside my car. He was cold and wet in the light rain falling that winter day. He wore a light windbreaker and looked tired. He had a suitcase and other bags in the cart.

I had a lot to do and was running late.

I drove past, but by the time I got to Staples I whipped my car around back in his direction. A nagging feeling in my gut told me to go back.

After asking him several questions and talking to him for a few moments, I decided it was safe to give him a ride to his house about a half mile away.

I helped load his stuff into the back of my car. As we headed out, I turned the heat on high because he was shivering.

What most people saw as they drove past the man was what I initially saw. Someone who might be dangerous. Someone who obviously had problems to be out pushing a shopping cart of his possessions in the rain.

What all those people who drove by would never know is that before he got sick the man made rocking chairs that are works of art and that he hoped he would be able to make them again.

He did have problems – health problems and apparently family problems. He told me he had been hospitalized. Upon discharge, family members were supposed to pick him up. They did not show up, so he loaded his stuff in a cart and headed for home.

I hope he is healthy again and able to make his beautiful rocking chairs.

I am glad I listened to "my gut" that day and took 15 minutes to help another human being.

I stopped giving rides to hitchhikers 30 years ago after Chip and I gave a person a ride that turned out to be very unnerving. I am, however, still willing to help people I do not know, and, in this case, give a ride to a stranger.

One time I gave a ride to a young man I did not know but who knew several people I know. I gave

178

him dry socks and shoes. He had been walking for days trying to get where he was going; his feet had been soaking wet for days and were in bad shape.

I was called crazy for doing this.

If crazy is helping another person in need and normal is ignoring the plight of other fellow beings, I will take crazy any day.

I hope the day never comes when I become so comfortable in my safe little world – or so fearful from all the horror stories in the news – that I am no longer willing to help another person who is having a rough time with life.

I hope the day never comes when I no longer see the divine spark that resides within every living creature.

If it had not been for the kindness of strangers during a rough time in my life, I might not be here today. If it had not been for a very few people I did know who believed in me even when I did not believe in myself, I might not be here today.

Thank you to the people who did not know me but gave me money for gas and paid a few dollars when I was short paying for my groceries. Thanks to the ones who gave me rides after I wrecked my car. And thanks to the person who "gave" me money saying they did not want repayment, they only wanted me to pay it forward.

I am paying it forward, even if people think I am crazy.

Acknowledgments

I am grateful to many who have encouraged me, believed in me, and supported me – helping me never to give up, well, maybe temporarily from time to time, but, so far, not permanently.

So many people. I am certain I will forget someone, so, in advance, I say "thank you" to you, too. Here is a list, in no particular order: Gilbert Edwards, Penny Smith, Carol Reuss, Jim Shumaker, Betty LaGrange, Loraye Hughes, Bob Morrison, Maxine Wright, Elizabeth Mitchell, Theresa Thompson, Tim Cranford, Pam Wiggins, Margaret Hodges Womick, Worth Womick, Mark Wayne Jordan, Timmy Womick, Serenity Rainbow Amber, Barry Campbell, Grady Womick, Jane Cassada, David and Dremia Meier, Isaac Needham, Kelso Coleman, Sebastian Ellington, Devin Routh, Carlton Cheek, Junior Lineberry, John Brooks, Lorene Brooks, Melissa Bentley, Sandy Pontius, Mary Murkin, Annette Jordan, Paul Church, Eric Abernethy, Kathi Keys, Bob Williams, Henry King, Megan Crotty, Martha Crotty, Jill Wood, Brittany N. Powers, Bob and Jackie Derr, Jane Braswell, Bobby Burns and Crystal Baity, Carol Sue Cummings Haught, Jon Megerian, Richard Meissner, William Neely, Charles Lewis, Jannell Curry, Laura Wulff, Bobby Edwards, Lawrence Perry, Kirsten Cox, Fred Graham, Harry Killian, Charles Stout, Phillip Scotton, Candie Rudzinski, Tommy McNeill, George Kivett, Robert Nixon, John Oravek, C.L. Hickerson, Marie Anderson-Whitehurst, Buster Otwell, Joey Hoskins, Don and Agnes Leonard, Julie Leonard, Reid Suggs, Jim Weston, Tink, Amanda, Stephanie, Ray Criscoe, Leslie Yow, Ruth and Henry Meier, Arthur and Beulah Jordan, Bernice Meier, Berrie Maxwell, Pandy McConnachie Kealy, Sherry Saunders, Barbara Tazewell, Emma Washington, Charlie Przybylowski, Michael Mahan, Mary Holmes, Dani Seip, Virginia Moore, Ginnie

Tate, Steve and Lee Tate, Dora Atlas, Dorothy Murray, Pamela McKinnon, Corliss Deese, Wes McCracken, Dan and Dedra Routh, Jay and Diane Hubbard, Jean Vollrath, Jessie Talbott, Marc Devokaitis, George and Lakita Adams, Debbie and Don Pickens, Dick and Joanne Peterson, Shelly Peterson, Dottie Lewis, Billie Nance, Susan Cavallier, Jacquie Reininger, Whit Roberson, Tim Matthews, Tommy Routh, Carrie and Bobby Bradds, Sarah, Beth, Geraldine, Mike, Rose Parson, Tova, the McGuires, especially Brenda and Breanna, Salvadore Tejeda and family, Wayne Cole, Guadalupe Gonzalez, Peter Nagel, Barbara, Susan, Ginger, and Scott Hunt, Stepahnie Ward Blum, Becky Faucette, Ann Shaw, Angela Nasab, Carl and Lynn Laughlin, Michelle McClain, Mike and Kay Tyson, Albert (the Blind Man), Richard and Faylene Whitaker, Ariel Davis Burroughs, Midge Noble, Roger Brown, Jimmy Brown, Jolie Corder, Robert Nixon, Matthew Schumaker, Ursula Hunsucker, Kevin Fox, Mike Fox, Ashlee Norwood and Mikaela, Bernadette and Lonnie Kornegay, Sandi Smith, Karen Red Glasses, Betsy Johnson, Kelly Link, Ben Grandon, Bonnie Unger, Valarie Snell, Peggy DeLay, Gayelynn Britt Phillips, Rahila Nargis, Michael Parris, "Helen" Ellen Morris, "Black Feather," Dwain Roberts, Jerry Earnhardt, Taylor Campbell, Mark Gross, Craig Parrish, Ronnie Kidd, Dustin Grant, Eldon Jackson, Stacy Letterlough and Evie, Jim McIntosh, Margaret Praigg, Martha Beudel, Roy Shoults, Deacon Plitt, Dumbass Red, Max Nunez, Jay and Emily Ledwell, Pam Mills, Ernie Mitchell, Warren and Sandra Dixon, Bob and Jen Daley, Lisa and David Overman, Beth Lester Winn.

Big Luv and a humongous thank you to Chip, who supported me, challenged me, and convinced me we needed to do this, when I did not feel I could possibly undertake the project of putting together a book. I really didn't. He did.

Another humongous thank you to the amazing Amber Mabe – who I am sure didn't know what she was getting into. I promise to learn to not be so neurotic by our next book.

Thank you to Diane Winnemuller, the former publisher at The Courier-Tribune in Asheboro, N.C., for permission to reprint these columns – which first appeared in the newspaper – in a future book.

Thank you to all the people (some I know but most were strangers) who helped me buy gas, cigarettes, food, and water – or gave me water or sunglasses or phone cords – at times in my life when I was wandering.

Thank you to the homeless people in Asheboro, N.C., who were some of the kindest people I've met – and who helped me keep hope alive during a really, dark time – because they let me help them.

To the narcissists and predators I have met along the way, I too am grateful. I am stronger because I survived you . . .

To my Creator, my guardian angel, the Archangel Gabriel, and *all* the angels, guides, fairies, animals, and plants who have been with me along the way – especially Digit, Strelly, Sky, Shadow, Ghost, and Lilly Wren – I give thanks.

Namaste.

"Be not forgetful to entertain strangers: for thereby some have entertained angels unawares.

Remember them that are in bonds, as bound with them; and them which suffer adversity, as being yourselves also in the body" (Hebrews 13: 2–3, King James Version).

CPSIA information can be obtained
at www.ICGtesting.com
Printed in the USA
BVHW081946110921
616355BV00001B/7

9 780997 166170